HOCKEY'S
GOLDEN ERA

HOCKEY'S
GOLDEN ERA
STARS OF THE ORIGINAL SIX

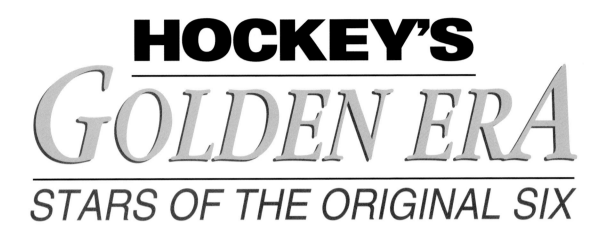

MIKE LEONETTI

Photographs from the Legendary

Harold Barkley Archives

Warwick Publishing Inc.

Toronto   Los Angeles

Published by the Warwick Publishing Group
Warwick Publishing Inc., 24 Mercer Street, Toronto, Ontario, M5V 1H3
Warwick Publishing Inc., 1300 Alexandria, Los Angeles, California, 90027

ISBN 1-895629-20-9

Distributed by:
Firefly Books Ltd.
250 Sparks Ave.,
Willowdale, Ontario
M2H 2S4

Printed and bound in Canada

Photographs by Harold Barkley. Photograph of Frank Selke on page 6 courtesy of the Hockey Hall of Fame.

*To the players, coaches and
managers of the "Golden Era"*

and

*to Harold Barkley,
hockey's greatest photographer*

FOREWORD

by Frank Selke, Jr.

When my father left the employ of the Toronto Maple Leafs and became General Manager of the Montreal Canadiens in 1946, I wheedled a job out of him on the Forum's maintenance crew, cleaning the ice, sweeping the seats, learning the arena business from the ice up — ultimately ending up in the early fifties as the English language Director of Public Relations for the famous Canadiens! I lived and worked in the "Golden Era." I knew the players, coaches and managers of all six teams. I met and listened to the greats of the game, Lester Patrick, Art Ross, Frank Boucher, Newsy Lalonde and that wonderful gentleman, Joe Malone, as they talked and reminisced about their years in the spotlight.

On many occasions I arranged for Hal Barkley to set up his cameras in the Forum, and many of the photos he took are before you now. I remember Hal as quiet and almost shy — his pictures did his talking. They spoke then and now with great eloquence

In 1960 I became the Hockey Night in Canada television studio host for games in Montreal, and over the next seven years I interviewed most of the players profiled in this book. Many of them are close friends to this day. What a delight it is to revisit them all again. The very nature of the six team NHL made each team a closely knit group. Rivalries were intense and volatile, yet through it all there was an obvious love of the game for its own sake, something we see much less of today.

There are wonderful memories for me in this book. Indeed, for anyone who watched these outstanding athletes "live" or on TV in the early days... or heard Foster Hewitt and Danny Gallivan on radio catch their wondrous skills and translate them into words... for anyone who experienced "Hockey's Golden Era," this book will recapture the exhilarating magic of those glorious days.

By bringing them back so vividly, Mike Leonetti and Hal Barkley remind me that, as good as today's stars are, we will never again see the likes of The Rocket, Big Gordie, the elegant Beliveau, the incredible Golden Jet, Terrible Ted Lindsay, young Bobby Orr and the many others who left indelible marks on the memory of anyone who saw them perform.

Here, between these pages is a richly deserved tribute to a time in hockey history that in my view, was indeed, the sport's golden era.

TABLE OF CONTENTS

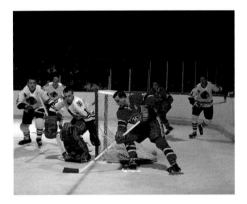

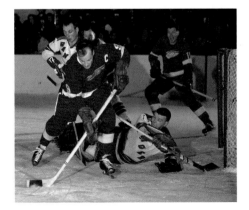

This book is not only about the great hockey players of the "Original Six" era, but also about another star who worked behind the scenes — Harold Barkley, the greatest hockey photographer of his day. Barkley was the first to shoot hockey games in colour, consequently, the images in this book started a revolution in hockey photography.

Barkley began shooting hockey games just after World War II. At that time all of the photographs were black & white because early colour films didn't have the exposure latitude to make hockey action photography practical. It wasn't until he began experimenting with electronic strobes that he was able to overcome the lighting problems that existed inside of hockey rinks.

Notice the flash units strategically placed along the glass in the background of the photograph to the right. Before game time, Barkley would set up these flash units and then wire them to his camera. The flash would be synchronized with his camera shutter, thus "stopping the action" and rendering photographs of incredible sharpness and detail.

Present day hockey and sports photography is normally taken with available arena lighting. The lighting is sufficient for modern day films, but because it is primarily "fill lighting" instead of "spot lighting" the photographs have a flat and dull quality. Compare that with Harold Barkley's shots which have a depth, and "three-dimensional" quality, that is not present in today's sports shots.

Of course, Barkley's method of photography required hours of lighting set-up, and resulted in only a few shots per game. Today's photographers do not have the time or equipment to operate that way. And that is precisely why you will never see Barkley's kind of photography again.

In addition to the technical revolution that Harold Barkley brought to sports photography, he was also a master at taking photos that put you right in the middle of the action. From a prime location, he had a way of catching the excitement of the game by freezing the superstars at their best

within the photo frame. His award winning work includes memorable shots of legends like Frank Mahovlich, Dave Keon, Jean Beliveau, Jacques Plante, Bobby Hull, Stan Mikita, Rod Gilbert, Johnny Bucyk and Bobby Orr. From the late Fifties

Right: Two legends of the game, Gordie Howe (9) and Terry Sawchuk , once teammates for Detroit, face each other deep in the Toronto zone.

to the end of the "Golden Era", Barkley brought us the game like nobody else. This book is a tribute to Mr. Barkley and his very distinguished work.

To accompany the fantastic photos, biographies of over 70 players who played with the "Original Six" have been compiled. The stories capture achievements and anecdotes on many of the stars who played in hockey's best era. Many of those featured are now in the Hockey Hall of Fame. A records and awards chapter at the end of the book provides a summary of the last decade, covering the final vestiges of a special time.

This book is not a "where are they now" anthology. Rather, it's a look back at the way they were then, highlighting heroes in their prime. Whether or not you're old enough to remember the days of the "Golden Era", this book will bring the "Original Six" to life for you. Enjoy the memories!

HOCKEY'S GOLDEN ERA

When the Brooklyn Americans dropped out of the National Hockey League for the 1942-43 season, it left six teams to compete for the Stanley Cup. The remaining clubs or the "original six" as they became known, stayed intact until the start of the 1967-68 season when the league doubled in size. The time between 1942 and 1967 has been called hockey's "Golden Era." Any hockey fan who was around in the days when the Toronto Maple Leafs, Montreal Canadiens, Chicago Blackhawks, Detroit Red Wings, New York Rangers and Boston Bruins made up the world's best league, will tell you what a special time it was. Someone who followed the game likely knew who all the players were because the NHL had only 120 jobs available. Players had to work very hard to make it into the league, and even harder to stay. Coaches and managers would not hesitate to bring in new people if any player lacked the drive required. It made for intense games and fierce rivalries between players and teams. Only the strong and skilled survived. Perhaps this is why a whole generation refers to players of the golden era as "heroes."

These heroes were brought to life for the fans in a variety of ways. Radio was the first medium to bring hockey directly into homes across the country. The play-by-play voice of Foster Hewitt crackled over the airwaves all across Canada. Every Saturday night his familiar "Hello, Canada and hockey fans in the United States" would signal the start of another epic battle that Hewitt would embellish at just the right moment. His phrases to describe the game became part of the hockey vernacular for years to come. Most Canadian youngsters gathered around the radio and dreamed of one day playing in Maple Leaf Gardens where Hewitt would describe their efforts to win the Stanley Cup! Many players in the golden era would recall the times they spent on a Saturday night listening to radio. It helped them to visualize their own goal of making it to the NHL.

The "Beehive Photos" provided by the St. Lawrence Starch Company, gave the fans a 5x7 black and white picture of their favourite player. All that was needed to collect these pictures was a proof of purchase. A hockey calendar from Maple Leaf Gardens or the Montreal Forum was often seen hanging in barbershops. They were a prized possession if you could get one for your home.

The neighbourhood store was not only a good place to hang out but the place to collect all kinds of hockey items. Bubble gum cards were the most popular, but you could also find coins in bags of potato chips, pictures available on pop bottle caps and colour shots on the back of cereal boxes. Getting "the set" was easier in those days because there were fewer players to worry about. All these items, and others, served as a connection between the fan and the player. In a simpler time, when owning a car was a status symbol and there was little inflation, fans collected because it was fun and it brought you closer to your hero. The monetary value of such items was totally irrelevant.

If there was one influence that fuelled the growth of hockey's golden era, it had to be television. "Hockey Night in Canada" made the transition from radio to television in 1952. It has been part of the Canadian culture ever since. On black and white televisions that didn't always work quite right, the fans could now actually see what Foster Hewitt had been describing. Soon people like Murray Westgate, Ward Cornell, Bill Hewitt, Jack Bennett, and Ed Fitkin would be familiar to people all across Canada on Toronto-based broadcasts. People who received the Montreal telecasts became familiar with broadcasters like Danny Gallivan, Dick Irvin Jr., Frank Selke Jr., and Rene Lecavalier (for the French network). In 1956-57, CBS Television started broadcasting games into the United States on Saturday afternoons.

Television helped to make stars out of players like Gordie Howe, Jean Beliveau, Frank Mahovlich, Rod Gilbert, Bobby Hull and Johnny Bucyk. Fans could now see a player's exploits on the ice and also have an opportunity to see his personality. The player could also be identified with his respective team because they were developed as a youngster by that club. Most of those who played in the golden era came to the NHL from a system where

Opposite: Toronto's Johnny Bower robs Bobby Hull in the goal mouth.

sponsorship played an important role. For example, everyone knew Mahovlich, having been developed in Toronto's junior system, would one day star with the Maple Leafs. Future Leafs were developed at St. Michael's High School or the Toronto Marboros while the Canadiens had their own junior club in Montreal. Hamilton served the Detroit Red Wings, Guelph did the job for the New York Rangers while Niagara Falls was the breeding spot for the Boston Bruins. Under this system a player could be tied to a team as soon as he became a teenager.

Although all six teams had a junior and minor league farm system to support the big club, they did not all enjoy the same level of success. Toronto, Montreal, and Detroit were able to achieve the most. Toronto won four Stanley Cups between 1947 and 1951. They also won four more Cups during the Sixties. George "Punch" Imlach took over a poor team in 1958 and kept the Leafs in contention for the Stanley Cup until 1968. Stanley Cup victories in 1962, 1963, 1964 and 1967 were a tribute to Imlach's coaching and managerial abilities. Building from the net out with goalie Johnny

Bower, Toronto's stout defense of Tim Horton, Bobby Baun and Allan Stanley was the backbone of four championship teams. Top forwards included Frank Mahovlich, Dave Keon, Red Kelly and George Armstrong. Not too concerned about the regular season, the Leafs always saved their best for the playoffs.

Montreal had the greatest dynasty in the history of hockey during the years 1956 to 1960. Under the masterful coaching of Hector "Toe" Blake, a bevy of stars like Doug Harvey, Maurice Richard, Jean Beliveau and Jacques Plante made the Canadiens Stanley Cup champions for five years in a row. They slipped a little in the early Sixties but came back to win the Cup in 1965, 1966, 1968 and 1969. Their new stars included J.C. Tremblay, Jacques Laperriere, John Ferguson and Bobby Rousseau. The Montreal winning tradition had been passed on to a new generation.

Built by Jack Adams, the Detroit Red Wings boasted two of hockey's all-time greats in Gordie Howe and Terry Sawchuk. Howe would prove to be the most durable player in hockey history, scoring 801 career goals. He also won the Hart Trophy six times. Sawchuk was the best goalie in the game over his long and illustrious career. He recorded 57 shutouts in his first five seasons and three Vezina Trophies in the same period. Detroit won four Stanley Cups between 1950 and 1955 but could only make it to the Finals during the Sixties. Four attempts at the Cup resulted in losses to Chicago, Toronto (twice) and Montreal.

The New York Rangers lost a heartbreaker in the 1950 Finals to Detroit in overtime of the seventh game. The Rangers had little playoff success for the rest of the Fifties. They did not fare much better in the early and mid-Sixties although they did have great players such as Andy Bathgate, Harry Howell, Rod Gilbert and Jean Ratelle. By 1967, the Rangers had rebuilt under Emile Francis to become a serious challenger.

The Fifties were good to the Boston Bruins with three trips to the Finals. However, the Sixties were a total disaster for the first seven years. Poor trades and a lack of young prospects kept Boston as cellar

dwellers with the New York Rangers between 1960 and 1967. A few Bruins like Johnny Bucyk, Ed Johnston and Ed Westfall stayed with the team long enough to see the good times which started in 1968. It was no coincidence of course that the Bruins' fortunes started to change when they added hockey's newest superstar, Bobby Orr. Listed as a defenseman, Orr controlled the tempo of any game he was in by playing superb hockey at both ends of the ice. His eight Norris Trophies and two Hart Trophies are a testament to his dominance. The game was never played the same way again after Orr made his mark on the league.

Orr's style of play was but one of many changes that hockey started to experience during the Sixties. For the most part, few players wore helmets unless they were recovering from injuries. Players were easy to identify with their neatly trimmed sideburns and crewcuts. However, players like Billy Harris, Red Kelly, Paul Henderson and Red Berenson started to wear the protective headgear on a regular basis. As time went on, the use of helmets became more and more popular.

Starting goalies rarely had a backup, and being cut by the puck simply meant that the game would be delayed until the goalie was stitched up. The starter always returned to the net whenever possible because coaches (especially the visitors) didn't want to use the "house goalie" sitting in the stands. Every home team was responsible for having an amateur standing by, waiting to go in if he had to. Such a situation was avoided by Montreal coach Toe Blake when he allowed Jacques Plante to play with a mask after his face had been ripped open by a shot. As the years passed, more and more goalies started to wear the mask although it took a surprisingly long time before they all did. Early pioneers with the mask, besides Plante, were Terry Sawchuk, Don Simmons and Charlie Hodge. For the 1963-64 season, the NHL passed a rule that all teams would have to carry two goalies.

Travel between the six NHL cities was primarily by train. Weekend games played on Saturday and Sunday nights would see the teams play, for example, in Toronto for the first game and in Detroit the following day. The teams would travel on the same train after the Saturday night game, and do their best to avoid each other. A chance meeting in the smoking or dining car could easily lead to fisticuffs. Such was the nature of the dislike teams had for one another. In later years teams began to recognize the advantages of plane travel. By the

Opposite: Two greats of the golden era —
Frank Mahovlich and Gordie Howe.

time expansion hit in 1967, travel by plane had become a necessity, and train travel abruptly came to a grinding halt.

In the mid-Sixties, a pair of high-scoring Blackhawks decided to try for an extra edge by bending the blades of their sticks to a wicked curve. Stan Mikita and Bobby Hull first developed their idea during practise. The "Banana Blade" sacrificed the backhand shot which required the tradi-tional straight stick. But, the curve would make the puck do funny things, giving goalies fits when they tried to follow the shot. Hard shooters like Hull found it could help them score more goals and it added an offensive weapon to what had been essentially a defensive game to that point.

In the Fifties and Sixties the game was largely based on goaltending and defense. The games usu-ally were low scoring with plenty of ties, and no

overtime to settle the issue. In 1962-63, the Montreal Canadiens finished the season with 23 ties! As a result it was not uncommon for goalies to have goals-against averages of under two per game. Shutouts were much more frequent as is evidenced by Terry Sawchuk's 103 career total which was accumulated between 1949 and 1970.

Scoring twenty goals was considered a very good, if not exceptional, season for most players. Between 1945 and 1967, the 50 goal barrier was hit by only three players – Maurice Richard, Bernie Geoffrion and Bobby Hull. When Hull scored his 51st goal in 1966 it was met with great celebration. Until Bobby Orr came along, the defenseman's role was primarily restricted to taking care of his own end. Some players like Doug Harvey, Pierre Pilote and Tim Horton could contribute to the offense with pinpoint passing and heavy shots, but were more concerned with defending their net. The games may have been lower scoring but they were fierce battles enjoyed greatly by the fans. In 1963-64, as the golden era was coming to an end, the NHL played to 94.5% capacity!

The six cities that made up the NHL were not the only locations that saw great hockey during the golden era. A number of minor leagues (like the American, International, Central, Western, Eastern Professional) saw future NHL players get their training. The minors provided most players with their first professional hockey experience and it prepared them for life in the NHL. Many cities that had minor league teams would one day join the NHL – Pittsburgh, St. Louis, Edmonton, Calgary, Winnipeg, Vancouver, Buffalo and Quebec City. Other key minor league cities included Rochester, Seattle, Providence, Springfield, Baltimore, Sudbury, San Francisco and Kingston. Because the hockey was so good, most of these operations were quite viable for a number of years.

Expansion came in 1966. The NHL announced it would double in size from six to 12 teams starting in 1967-68. It signalled the end of the golden era and the face of hockey would change forever. Soon fans would have trouble remembering all the play-er's names and what team they played for. Players would now be "drafted" into the league. Gone was sponsorship, and with it went Montreal's ability to get the top prospects in Quebec, and Toronto's chance to grab the best of what Ontario produced. No longer would NHLers play with the severe injuries they once did. No more Bobby Bauns skating out on a cracked ankle to score a winning goal in the playoffs! Players could now afford to take a night off. Fighting would never again be seen as a healthy way for two men to settle a dispute. It would now be a "violent" aspect of the game.

The all-star game format of the Stanley Cup champion hosting a team of league stars in October would be changed for an East-West game in January! The Stanley Cup would never be decided in the month of April again. Clarence Campbell, NHL president between 1946 and 1977, would not be able to rule over the game with an iron fist. Also gone were the 14 meetings between teams where a real hatred could be built up over the course of a 70 game season. For these and many other reasons, hockey would never be the same again.

The golden era had one last hurrah in 1967 when the Toronto Maple Leafs and the Montreal Canadiens met for the Stanley Cup. It was only fitting that hockey's greatest rivalry would conclude the era of the "original six." It was a classic match-up featuring Toronto's over-the-hill gang against the Flying Frenchmen. Behind the superb goaltending of Johnny Bower and Terry Sawchuk, the Leafs took a 3 - 2 series lead back to Maple Leaf Gardens for game six. Toronto was up 2 - 1 with under a minute to go, when coach Punch Imlach sent out five veterans to protect Sawchuk against six Canadiens. Very cooly, the Leafs executed a perfect play from a face-off in their own end. Leaf captain George Armstrong crossed the center redline before depositing a shot into the empty Montreal net to clinch the Stanley Cup for Toronto. The Leafs-Canadiens series provided an enduring image of hockey's greatest era and of a time we will not see again.

Opposite: J.C. Tremblay and goalie Charlie Hodge cover up against the Boston Bruins.

BOSTON BRUINS

The Boston Bruins were a successful team during the decade of the Fifties when they missed the playoffs just once and made it to the Finals three times. In 1953, 1957 and 1958 the Bruins lost the Stanley Cup to the Montreal Canadiens. It was difficult to stop the Canadiens who were in the middle of a dynasty. The Bruins were a good skating team that used its size to make up for a little less talent. However, after a Semi-Final loss to Toronto in 1959, the Bruins started to move some players out. As a result the team settled into a long slumber of sixth place finishes.

Between the years of 1960 and 1967, the Bruins finished out of the playoffs for eight consecutive years and were the worst team in the NHL six times. The Bruins shared the basement of the league during the Sixties with the New York Rangers. Boston appeared to have a long term lease on sixth place and on five occasions recorded less than 20 victories in a 70 game season.

Some Bruin problems were clear for all to see. The lack of a quality goaltender haunted them when they no longer had Don Simmons and Harry Lumley. They acquired Terry Sawchuk in 1955 from Detroit and thought he would be their goalie for a long time. But in 1957, Sawchuk was returned to the Red Wings when he could not adjust to playing in Boston. Until Ed Johnston was able to team up with Gerry Cheevers, the Bruins used goalies like Don Head, Jim Norris, Ed Chadwick, Bobby Perreault and Bruce Gamble.

Over time, the Bruins became a small team that lacked enough fire power on the forward lines. They did try to play an aggressive game with players like Ted Green, Leo Boivin, Forbes Kennedy, Orland Kurtenbach, Reggie Fleming and Johnny McKenzie. The Bruins fans appreciated a tough game and kept the arena filled even through the losing seasons.

The Bruins did have some great players during this bleak period, most notably scoring wingers in Johnny Bucyk, Doug Mohns, Bronco Horvath, Vic Stasiuk and Tom Williams. Top centers in-

Right: Ed Johnston (1) searches for the puck through a maze of Bruin and Leaf players.

cluded, Murray Oliver and Pit Martin. Leo Boivin was the league's most feared bodychecker and Ted Green was a tough customer. Goalie Ed Johnston proved he could handle the NHL job by playing in every game in 1963-64.

Boston management tried to help these players by acquiring seasoned veterans like Leo Labine, Jerry Toppazzini, Andre Pronovost, Fern Flaman, Ron Stewart, Dean Prentice, Andy Hebenton and Parker MacDonald. None of these additions lasted very long, but the Bruins did have one glorious night in their seasons of misery. In February, 1964 the Bruins whipped the Stanley Cup champions, the Toronto Maple Leafs 11 - 0 right in Maple Leaf Gardens on a Saturday night!

Predictably, the Bruins went through a few coaches and there was upheaval in the general manager's office. Lynn Patrick, Hap Emms and Milt Schmidt took turns running the Bruins in the front office and behind the bench. After a change in plans, Emms was gone and Schmidt once again took over as the general manager. This time he would make changes that would see the Bruins rise to be one of the league powers.

In part, Schmidt's second attempt at running the Bruins was successful because the farm system started to produce some young quality players. Boston youngsters included Don Awrey, Dallas Smith, Gary Dornhoefer, Wayne Cashman, Bernie Parent, Gilles Marotte, Ed Westfall and Pat

Stapleton. These young players mixed in with veterans like Green, Bucyk, Williams and Johnston. The Bruins lost some of the young players in the expansion draft of 1967, while others were traded away to bring in better players. In fact, one deal changed the face of the Bruin team in May, 1967.

Needing a bigger and more aggressive team, Schmidt acquired Phil Esposito, Ken Hodge and Fred Stanfield from Chicago. It was one of the most one-sided deals in the history of hockey, with Boston giving up Pit Martin, Gilles Marotte and Jack Norris in return. The Bruins started to roll and would crush teams like Toronto and Detroit by 1968-69. Soon they found themselves on top of the league with Montreal and their old basement partners, the New York Rangers.

The most notable addition to the Bruins was defenseman Bobby Orr. The game of hockey was never the same after Orr made his first appearance for Boston in 1966-67. He revolutionized the defenseman's role and the game of hockey produced more offense than ever before with the Bruins leading the way. Orr won the Norris Trophy a remarkable eight years in a row.

Under the coaching of Harry Sinden, the Bruins won the Stanley Cup in 1970. Sinden abruptly left the team but the Bruins bounced back to win the Cup again in 1972. Sinden returned to Boston early in the 1972-73 season as the general manager. The Bruins have not missed the playoffs since!

Opposite: Ed Westfall celebrates scoring
on Detroit's Terry Sawchuk.

LEO BOIVIN

For Leo Boivin, dishing out a good body check was just as satisfying as scoring a goal. Sturdily built at 5'9" and 190 pounds, Boivin was a strong believer in playing the man, not the puck. He was a textbook hitter, delivering a clean, hard belt usually in open ice. A Boivin check could stop an opponent dead in his tracks and force him to keep his head up the rest of the game. His hits may have been hard, but they were clean as evidenced by the fact that Boivin recorded 100 penalty minutes in only one of his 19 NHL seasons!

The stocky defenseman began his NHL career in Toronto where he played two seasons for the Leafs. Toronto manager Conn Smythe decided to send Boivin to Boston in exchange for Joe Klukay in November, 1954. He finished the 1954-55 season with Boston scoring six goals and 17 points while recording 105 penalty minutes. He joined Boston at just the right time.

In both 1957 and 1958 the Bruins made it all the way to the Stanley Cup Finals before losing to the Montreal Canadiens. A year later, the Bruins were knocked off in seven games by Toronto in the 1959 Semi-Finals and a dark era began in Boston. Although he was named captain in 1963,

Boivin would never make the playoffs again with the Bruins. He did get another chance at the Stanley Cup when he was dealt to Detroit in 1966. The Red Wings lost in the Finals to the Canadiens.

Boivin was taken by Pittsburgh in the 1967 expansion draft and he played his 1000th NHL game for the Penguins. He was traded to Minnesota where he played two more years before he retired. He stayed in hockey as a scout and then as coach of the St. Louis Blues for a couple of seasons.

His long career was rewarded in 1986 when he was elected to the Hall of Fame.

Born: 8/2/32, Prescott, Ontario.					
Height: 5'7" Weight: 190 Shot: Left Position: Defense					
Sweater # 20 Years Played: 1951 - 1970					
Teams: Toronto, Boston, Detroit, Pittsburgh, Minnesota					
	GP	G	A	PTS	PM
	1150	72	250	322	1137
Playoffs:	54	3	10	13	59

Above: Leo Boivin moves in for a shot on Toronto's goalie Johnny Bower.

Right: Boivin played for five NHL teams in his career.

JOHNNY BUCYK

In July, 1957 the Detroit Red Wings reacquired goalie Terry Sawchuk from Boston in exchange for left winger Johnny Bucyk. Since Bucyk had received such little ice time from the Red Wings, many wondered who he was and why the Bruins would want him. He was much better known in his native Edmonton where he starred in the Western Hockey League as the rookie of the year in 1954-55. His play in the minors earned him a spot on the Red Wings team for the 1955-56 season. Soon the fans in the Boston Garden would know who Bucyk was, and that he could score goals.

Bucyk responded to the challenge and scored 21 and 24 goals in his first two seasons in Boston. Playing on what was dubbed the "Uke Line" with Bronco Horvath and Vic Stasiuk, Bucyk also recorded point totals of 52 and 60. He helped Boston to the Finals in 1958 and the Semi-Finals in 1959 before a long drought began for the Bruins. From 1960 to 1967, Boston failed to make the playoffs each season although Bucyk managed to score over 20 goals on four separate occasions during those years. His best season was in 1962-63 when he scored 27 goals and had 66 points.

Left: Johnny Bucyk became a 50-goal scorer for the Bruins.

Right: Bucyk (9) chases New York's Doug Harvey (2).

By staying through the tough times, Bucyk was able to enjoy being a Bruin when the situation started to improve. In 1967-68, the Bruins made the playoffs and Bucyk netted 30 goals, earning him a berth on the second all-star team. As the Boston powerhouse gathered steam under Bobby Orr and Phil Esposito, Bucyk was named captain of the team and became known as "Chief." After a Stanley Cup victory in 1970, Bucyk had the best year of his career in 1970-71 when he scored 51 goals and 116 points. He was named to the first all-star team and was awarded the Lady Byng Trophy.

In 1972, Bucyk was presented with the Stanley Cup for the second time in three years when Bos-ton defeated the New York Rangers in six games. Bucyk played with the Bruins until 1978 and was elected to the Hall of Fame in 1981.

	Born: 5-12-1935, Edmonton, Alberta				
	Height: 6' Weight: 215 Shot: Left Position: Left Wing				
	Sweater # 9 Years Played: 1958 - 1978				
	Teams: Detroit, Boston				
	GP	G	A	PTS	PM
	1540	566	813	1369	497
Playoffs:	124	41	62	103	42

TED GREEN

When Boston general manager Lynn Patrick was looking for a successor to tough guy Fern Flaman, he spotted young Ted Green who was playing with the Winnipeg Warriors of the Western Hockey League. In June, 1960 Patrick took the opportunity to draft Green from the Montreal Canadiens (who owned his playing rights very briefly) and the Bruins had a new leader for their blueline corps.

Green opened the 1961-62 season in Boston and led the team with 116 penalty minutes. He broke his hand trying to get at Toronto's Frank Mahovlich. It was just one of many scraps he would take part in as a rookie. Displaying a short fuse and a willingness to use his fists, Green recorded over 100 penalty minutes in his first five NHL seasons with Boston. He needed to be physical since the Bruins were not one of the bigger teams in the league. Green forced the opposition to keep their heads up in the Bruin end of the ice.

Through sheer determination Green's play steadily improved. A good shot blocker, Green was also used as a forward to kill penalties which gave him more confidence. He was effective at carrying the puck and showed he could handle the point position for the Bruins. His abrasive style led to some injuries, but when Green played full seasons he recorded assist totals of 27, 36, 38 and 37. He had his best year in 1968-69 when he was named

to the NHL's second all-star team, scoring eight goals and 46 points.

In September, 1969 Green suffered a serious head injury due to a stick swinging incident. He missed the entire 1969-70 season and was considered lucky to be alive. He showed great heart, character and determination to make a miraculous return to the NHL in 1970-71, recording 42 points for the Bruins. Green finally received the ultimate reward for a hockey player when he was a part of the Boston team that won the Stanley Cup in 1972.

An assistant coach with Edmonton for five Stanley Cups, Green was named head man of the Oilers in 1991.

		Born: 3-23-1940, Eriksdale, Manitoba			
Height: 5'10"		Weight: 200 Shot: Right Position: Defense			
	Sweater # 6	Years Played: 1960 - 1972			
		Teams: Boston			
	GP	G	A	PTS	PM
	620	48	206	254	1029
Playoffs:	31	4	8	12	54

Above: Ted Green eludes Dave Keon of Toronto.

Opposite: Always aggressive, Green (6) takes Montreal's Henri Richard (16) out of the play.

EDDIE JOHNSTON

Eddie Johnston was the last goalie in NHL history to play a full schedule for his team. Johnston was in the nets for all 70 Boston Bruin games in the 1963-64 season. On a poor team that only won 18 times, Johnston was still able to record six shutouts. He did all of this in only his second season!

The Montreal native played junior hockey in the Canadiens system where his best year was in 1960-61 when he played for the Hull-Ottawa Canadiens of the EPHL. He was named the league's top goalie and had 11 shutouts. Johnston also played in Winnipeg, Shawinigan Falls, Edmonton and Spokane. The Boston Bruins were impressed and drafted Johnston from Montreal in June, 1962.

In his first year in Boston, Johnston played in 49 games and had one shutout for a last place club. He had a variety of backup partners including Jack Norris and Bernie Parent until the Bruins settled on Gerry Cheevers. Cheevers was the more flashy

of the two and helped take pressure off Johnston who relied on his game of playing the angles.

The Bruins gambled that Johnston and Cheevers would lead the team to the Stanley Cup and left the promising Parent and Doug Favell up for grabs in the 1967 expansion draft. The gamble was a good one for Boston as they won two Stanley Cups. In the 1972 playoffs, Johnston's 1.86 goals against average was the best among the goalies.

	Born: 11-24-1935, Montreal, Quebec					
	Height: 6' Weight:190 Shot: Left Position: Goalie					
	Sweater # 1 Years Played: 1962 - 1978					
	TEAMS: Boston, Toronto, St. Louis, Chicago					
	GP	W	L	T	AVG	SO
	591	236	256	87	3.25	32
Playoffs:	18	7	10	-	3.34	1

In 1973, Johnston was dealt to Toronto where he played one season before he was sent to St. Louis. He was sold to Chicago in January, 1978 where he finished his career at the age of 42.

One of the last goalies to play without a mask, Johnston only donned the protection after teammate Bobby Orr hit him in the head with a shot during a pre-game warmup.

Opposite: Ed Johnston played in all 70 games for Boston in 1963-64.

Below: Johnston (1) stops the Rangers' Andy Hebenton (12) in close.

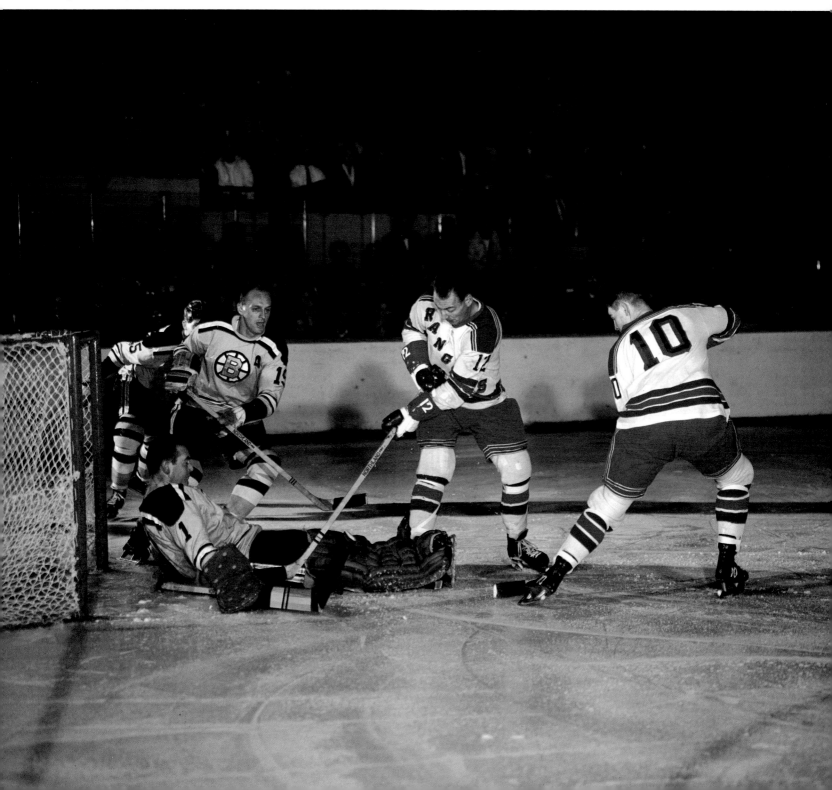

DOUG MOHNS

Doug Mohns will be remembered as a very versatile performer in a career that lasted 22 years with five different teams. Mohns could play both left wing and defense making him a big asset for every team he played on. Switching roles probably cost him a little personal recognition but he was always willing to help the team in whatever role was necessary.

Mohns was only 19 years old when he made it to the NHL. His potential was considered quite high because he was a great skater and shooter. He came to the Boston Bruins after winning the Memorial Cup with the Barrie Flyers of the OHA. In his last season of junior, the left winger scored 34 goals and 76 points in just 56 games. He played his

first year in Boston during the 1953-54 season without any time in the minor leagues. He managed 13 goals and 27 points as a rookie.

After three years as a forward, the Bruins decided to give Mohns a shot at defense. Working from the blueline, Mohns could take advantage of his excellent speed while carrying the puck out of his own end. He also displayed a terrific point shot. The move paid off big in 1959-60 when Mohns potted 20 goals and had 45 points.

Tired of playing on a losing team, Mohns was not too upset when he was traded to Chicago in June, 1964. Eventually he was made a member of the "Scooter Line" with Stan Mikita and Ken Wharram. He had his best season in 1966-67 when he scored 25 goals and had 35 assists to help Chicago finish first.

The Blackhawks were much better than the Bruins but Mohns' only Stanley Cup Final appearance was a loss to Montreal in 1965.

Chicago sent him to Minnesota in 1971 before Atlanta took him in the 1972 expansion draft. He was named the first ever captain of the Washington Capitals for his last NHL season in 1974-75.

	Born: 12-13-1933, Capreol, Ontario				
	Height: 6' Weight: 184 Shot: Left Position: Defense				
	Teams: Boston, Chicago, Minnesota, Atlanta, Washington				
	Sweater # 19 Years Played: 1953 - 1975				
	GP	G	A	PTS	PM
	1390	248	462	710	1230
Playoffs:	94	14	36	50	122

Opposite: Mohns played both forward and defense for the Bruins.

Below: Doug Mohns (19) upends the Rangers' Camille Henry (21) with some help from Charlie Burns (10).

MURRAY OLIVER

Murray Oliver turned down an offer to play professional baseball with the Cleveland Indians. Instead he opted to keep developing as a hockey player in Hamilton, Ontario, his home town. Playing for the Hamilton Tiger-Cubs of the OHA, Oliver won the Red Tilson Memorial Trophy (league MVP) for his play in 1957-58 when he had 34 goals and 90 points in 52 games. He then played for Edmonton of the WHL for a season and a half before being promoted to the Detroit Red Wings.

As center for his idol Gordie Howe, Oliver scored 20 goals in 54 games in 1959-60. After play-

ing in 46 games for Detroit the following year, he was traded to Boston in January, 1961. The Bruins gave up two good players in Leo Labine and Vic Stasiuk to get the smallish Oliver. He might not have been big but he was a consistent player who was always hustling on the ice. He had a good shot, a quick stride and worked hard to develop his playmaking skills.

In Boston, Oliver produced three consecutive seasons of more than 20 goals. Playing on a line with Johnny Bucyk and Tommy Williams, Oliver enjoyed his greatest season in 1963-64 when he had 24 goals. His 68 point total put him seventh overall in the league scoring race despite playing for a poor team. He was one of the few bright spots for Boston that year.

His production slipped to nine goals in 1966-67 and the Bruins decided they wanted to get bigger players on the team. As a result Oliver was dealt to Toronto for Eddie Shack in May, 1967. He played two years for the Leafs before they traded him to Minnesota. Oliver played five years with the North Stars recording a career high 27 goals in 1971-72.

Oliver turned to coaching after he retired and in 1982-83 he was behind the North Star bench for a total of 36 games as head coach.

Born: 11-14-1937, Hamilton, Ontario				
Height: 5'9" Weight: 170 Shot: Left Position: Center				
Sweater # 16 Years Played: 1957 - 1975				
Teams: Detroit, Boston, Toronto, Minnesota				
GP	G	A	PTS	PM
1127	274	454	728	356
Playoffs: 35	9	16	25	10

Left: Oliver (16) searches for a rebound after taking a shot on Toronto's goalie Terry Sawchuk. Tim Horton (7) and Allan Stanley (25) are defending.

Right: Murray Oliver played on the Bruins top line with Johnny Bucyk and Tom Williams.

BOBBY ORR

In their never ending search for talent, the Boston Bruins brain trust of Weston Adams, Wren Blair, Lynn Patrick and Milt Schmidt were out scouting a couple of prospects in Ontario. Afterwards they all agreed that the best player they saw was neither of the two prospects they came to watch, but a kid from Parry Sound, Ontario, named Bobby Orr. When Blair completed a masterful sales presentation to the Orr family, the Bruins' hunt for a superstar was finally over. In 1962-63, a 14 year-old Orr suited up for the Oshawa Generals, the Bruins affiliate in the OHA.

Orr started earning headlines in Oshawa and was quickly labelled as the Bruins' saviour. On defense for the Generals, Orr's goal totals read 29, 34 and 38 in three full seasons. Such numbers were unheard of for defensemen in those days. Small at first, Orr grew to a sturdy 5'11" and 180 pounds. He could take and give out punishment equally well. At the age of 18 he was ready for the NHL.

In 1966-67, playing for a last place club, Orr won the rookie of the year award even though he missed a number of games due to a knee injury. He played in 61 games, scoring 13 times and adding 28 assists. The Bruins made some key acquisitions (Phil Esposito, Ken Hodge, Fred Stanfield) and started to roll under Orr's leadership and dominance. In typical Orr fashion, he seized the opportunity to score the Stanley Cup winning goal in

1970 during overtime against the St. Louis Blues. He also scored the Stanley Cup winner in 1972.

By the time his career was over, Orr had won the Hart Trophy three times and was a double winner of both the Art Ross and the Conn Smythe. Winning the Norris Trophy eight years in a row was a clear indication of how he controlled the game whenever he stepped on the ice. Orr's speed, acceleration and spectacular rushes made him hockey's greatest attraction. His great shot and sense of anticipation allowed him to score virtually at will.

Due to injuries Orr's time in the NHL was relatively short but his impact on the game was revolutionary.

Born: 3-20-1948, Parry Sound, Ontario					
Height: 6' Weight: 199 Shot: Right Position: Defense					
Sweater # 4 Years Played: 1966 - 1979					
Teams: Boston, Chicago					
	GP	G	A	PTS	PM
	657	270	645	915	953
Playoffs:	74	26	66	92	107

Above: Bobby Orr was named the league's top rookie in 1967.

Opposite: Orr won the Norris Trophy as best defenseman eight years in a row.

ANDY HEBENTON

Above: Andy Hebenton (12) skates away from Toronto's Frank Mahovlich.

During his debut season with the New York Rangers in 1955-56, Andy Hebenton played in all 70 games and scored 24 goals. He would stay with the New York for the next eight seasons, scoring over 20 goals a total of five times. In just his second season, Hebenton scored 21 goals and 44 points and was named winner of the Lady Byng Trophy. His best goal scoring total was 33 in 1958-59. He did not miss a single game in his entire stay in New York.

Despite his durability, Hebenton was left unprotected by the Rangers and he was claimed by the Boston Bruins in the intra-league draft of 1963. Hebenton once again played in all 70 games for the Bruins giving him a career total of 560 consecutive appearances. It set a new NHL mark which would last until the Seventies when it was broken by Garry Unger. Considering that Hebenton did not shy away from body contact, his consecutive game record was amazing. He was not afraid to go into the corners and was thought of as a good backchecker.

	Born: 10-3-1929, Winnipeg, Manitoba				
Height: 5'9" Weight: 182 Shot: Right Position: Defense					
Sweater # 12 Years Played: 1955 - 1964					
Teams: New York Rangers, Boston					
	GP	G	A	PTS	PM
	630	189	202	391	83
Playoffs:	22	6	5	11	8

TOM JOHNSON

Above: Tom Johnson (10) moves in to check Detroit's Gordie Howe (9) as Goalie Eddie Johnston reaches for the puck.

The Boston Bruins raised a few eyebrows when they drafted defenseman Tom Johnson from the Montreal Canadiens in June, 1963. Recovering from a serious eye injury the previous year, Johnson came back to play in all 70 games for Boston in 1963-64 and had 25 points. One hockey publication named him as the come-back player of the year. The Bruins' investment had paid off.

In Montreal, Johnson played in the shadow of Doug Harvey. However, in 1958-59 he received the recognition due him by winning the Norris Trophy and breaking Harvey's hold on the top defenseman award. Johnson was also named to the first all-star team that year, recording a career high 10 goals and 39 points. He was on six Stanley Cup winning teams with Montreal and proved himself to be a great competitor over the years.

Named to the Hall of Fame in 1970, Johnson became coach of the Bruins in 1970-71 with Boston losing only 14 games in his first season behind the bench. The following year, 1971-72, Johnson coached the Bruins to a Stanley Cup victory.

Born: 2-18-1928, Baldur, Manitoba					
Height: 6' Weight: 180 Shot: Left Position: Defense					
Sweater # 10 Years Played: 1947 - 1965					
Teams: Montreal, Boston					
	GP	G	A	PTS	PM
	978	51	213	264	960
Playoffs:	111	8	15	23	109

DON McKENNEY

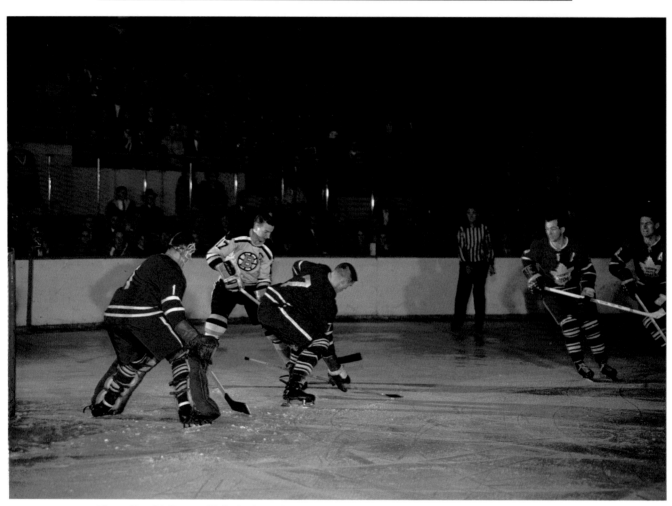

Above: Don McKenny (17) looks for a shot at Toronto goalie Don Simmons (1), as Tim Horton defends.

Don McKenney was a very steady and clean hockey player throughout his NHL career. He excelled in his first season with the Boston Bruins in 1954-55 by scoring 22 goals and 42 points, and his play reminded some of former Bruin great Bill Cowley.

McKenney came to the Bruins after playing only 54 games in the minors with the Hershey Bears. The 6' tall winger quickly established himself as a good two-way player. In nine years with Boston, McKenney recorded eight seasons of 20 or more goals. He led the Bruins in goals scored on three occasions including a career high 32 in 1958-59 when he played on a line with Leo Labine and Jerry Toppazzini. In 1959-60, McKenney led the NHL in assists with 49 and had a career best 69 points. He was also awarded the Lady Byng Tro-

phy for his gentlemanly play. McKenney was a valuable playoff performer scoring 17 points in 12 games during the 1958 post-season when Boston lost in the Finals to Montreal. He was named captain of the Bruins in 1961.

Born: 4-30-1934, Smith Falls, Ontario
Height: 6'   Weight: 175   Shot: Left   Position: Defense
Sweater # 17   Years Played: 1954 - 1968
Teams: Boston, New York Rangers, Toronto, Detroit, St. Louis

	GP	G	A	PTS	PM
	798	237	356	593	248
Playoffs:	58	18	29	47	10

ED WESTFALL

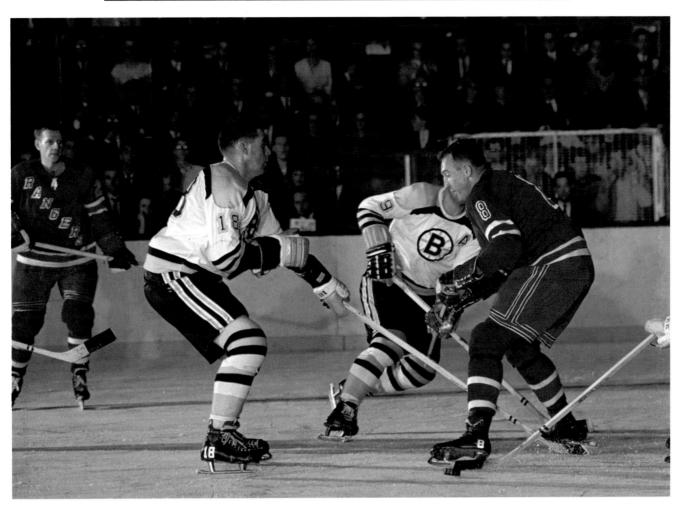

Above: Ed Westfall (18) checks the Rangers' Bob Nevin (8).

After his first season in the NHL in 1961-62 with the Boston Bruins, Ed Westfall was returned to the minors to develop his skills with a little less pressure on him. In Kingston, his coach, Harry Sinden moved Westfall from defense to right wing. He learned the skills necessary to be a checking forward. A role as a shadow awaited him back in Boston as the struggling Bruins tried to rebuild.

Westfall stayed with the Bruins for good in 1964-65 when he played in 68 games and scored 12 goals. The Bruins started to add new and better players, including Westfall's center, the feisty Derek Sanderson. The pair became great penalty killers and played a big role on two Boston Stanley Cup teams in 1970 and 1972. In 1970-71, Westfall scored over 20 goals for the first time in his career when he

notched 25. He also had a total of 59 points for his best year as a Bruin.

Westfall's perseverance and dedication to hockey were recognized when he was awarded the Masterton Trophy in 1977 while playing with his last NHL team, the New York Islanders.

Born: 9-19-1940, Belleville, Ontario
Height: 6'1" Weight: 197 Shot: Right Position: Right Wing
Sweater Number # 1 Years Played: 1961 - 1979
Teams: Boston, New York Islanders

	GP	G	A	PTS	PM
	1227	231	394	625	544
Playoffs:	95	22	37	59	41

CHICAGO BLACKHAWKS

By the mid-Fifties, the Chicago Blackhawks were nearly out of business. The franchise was not making any money and attendance had declined to the point where the Blackhawks would play regular season home games in cities like St. Louis, Omaha and St. Paul. A big reason for the Blackhawks' struggle was their poor record on the ice. Between 1947 and 1957 Chicago finished last nine times and missed the playoffs 11 of 12 years.

The NHL was so concerned about the status of the Chicago team that a plan was devised to help the Blackhawks with players from other teams. Under the "save the Blackhawks" plan, the Chicago team received players from other NHL teams. While they were not given any great players (some were considered trouble makers by their previous club for union activities), the Blackhawks did get some good talent like Eddie Litzenberger from the Canadiens. Litzenberger won the Calder Trophy and would later be named captain.

In addition to the players donated by the other teams, the Blackhawks took steps of their own to improve. First, owner Jim Norris sank $2 million into the team and then hired a capable hockey man in Tommy Ivan to run the club. Ivan came from the Detroit organization where he had coached the Red Wings to three Stanley Cup victories. Moving into a management role, Ivan realized he had to rebuild the Chicago team through the farm system. Using their junior squad in St. Catherines and their minor league team in Buffalo, Ivan began to realize the benefits of developing players.

During the late Fifties, the system produced such gems as Bobby Hull, Stan Mikita, Bill Hay, Elmer Vasko, Ken Wharram, Murray Balfour, Pierre Pilote and Chico Maki. Ivan also showed a good eye when making deals by acquiring all-star goalie Glenn Hall, defensemen Dollard St. Laurent and Jack Evans and forwards like Ron Murphy, Ab McDonald, Eric Nestrenko and Reggie Fleming. In 1957, Ivan promoted Rudy Pilous from the junior team in St. Catherines to coach the big team in Chicago. In 1958-59, the Blackhawks finally made the playoffs, and then again in 1959-60.

Right: Chicago's goalie Glenn Hall moves out to challenge a shooter. Eric Nesterenko (15) and Wayne Hillman (20) look on.

In 1960-61, Chicago finished in third place winning a club record 29 games. They saved their best for the playoffs when they ended Montreal's five year reign in a six game Semi-Final. The key game in the series with the Canadiens was the third, played at the Chicago Stadium. Some observers have called it one of the greatest games in playoff history. Chicago finally won it 2 - 1 on a goal by Murray Balfour in the third overtime period!

The 1961 Cup Finals were an all-American affair (the only one in the decade of the Sixties) between the Red Wings and the Blackhawks, with Chicago winning in five games. They won the last game 5 - 1 with Ab McDonald scoring the winning goal. The Blackhawks had gone from near extinction to winning hockey's most coveted prize. It was only the third time Chicago had won the Stanley Cup.

In the remaining years of the Sixties, the Blackhawks never missed the playoffs. In 1966-67, the Blackhawks made more team history by finishing first in the regular season. They won 41 games and finished with 94 points under coach Billy Reay who had replaced Pilous in 1963. It was the first time Chicago had the best record in the NHL. A second Stanley Cup appeared imminent, but the upstart Maple Leafs knocked off the Blackhawks in the Semi-Finals. Chicago returned to the Finals in 1971 and 1973 but lost both times to Montreal.

Many have wondered why a team as talented

as the Blackhawks did not win more Stanley Cups. They had hockey's greatest star of the Sixties in Bobby Hull and some excellent talent in Glenn Hall, Stan Mikita and Pierre Pilote. Hull was a natural goal scorer who could lift the crowd out of their seats with his rushes down the wing, or when unleashing a blast with his slapshot. He was the first player to score over 50 goals in a season. Mikita was a consistent point producer when he decided to stay out of the penalty box. He won the Art Ross Trophy four times and later became a multiple winner of the Lady Byng and the Hart.

Glenn Hall and Pierre Pilote took care of the Blackhawks own end. Hall was perhaps the biggest reason Chicago won the Cup in 1961. He won the Vezina Trophy in 1963 with the Blackhawks and was named to the first all-star team seven times over his entire career. Pilote was an eight time all-star and a winner of the Norris Trophy three years in a row between 1963 and 1965.

Unfortunately for the Blackhawks, they could never find the right mix again. The lack of good role players was the major weakness in Chicago lineup, and despite having some great players, they had to settle for only one championship year.

Above: Coach Rudy Pilous took the Chicago Blackhawks to the Stanley Cup in 1961

Opposite: Known as the "Golden Jet," Bobby Hull eludes Toronto's Bobby Baun.

GLENN HALL

For a man who became ill before he went out and did his job, goalie Glenn Hall performed remarkably well. Being a netminder was a joyless job for Hall who was a quiet and intense individual. It is ironic that one of Hall's NHL records includes playing in 502 consecutive games when you consider he disliked the work.

Hall started playing in goal as a bantam in Humboldt, Saskatchewan because no one else wanted to play in net. He would have preferred to play as a forward, but once he started to have success as a goalie he stayed with it and developed his skills. He turned professional in the Detroit organization, playing his first year with Indianapolis of the AHL in 1951-52. He spent three seasons with Edmonton of the WHL before making it to the Red Wings in 1955-56. He played a full 70 game schedule, posting a 2.11 goals-against average and an amazing 12 shutouts. He was also awarded the Calder Trophy as best rookie.

Although Detroit had traded Terry Sawchuk to Boston to make room for him, Red Wings coach Jack Adams didn't like the way Hall played in the playoffs. Detroit decided to get Sawchuk back and traded Hall to the Chicago Blackhawks in July, 1957. In his first game for Chicago, Hall recorded a 1-0 win over Toronto on a goal by Ted Lindsay who had been sent to the Blackhawks in the same deal.

With Hall in net, Chicago's fortunes started to rise and they won the Stanley Cup in 1961 by defeating Detroit in six games. Before beating Detroit, Chicago ended Montreal's five-year reign by knocking off the mighty Canadiens in the Semi-Finals. In the final game against Montreal, Hall recorded a 3-0 shutout.

The first goalie to use the butterfly style, Hall was an 11 time all-star and a three time winner of the Vezina Trophy. "Mr. Goalie" also won the Conn Smythe Trophy for his brillant performance with the St. Louis Blues in the 1968 playoffs.

Born: 10-3-1931, Humboldt, Saskatchewan						
Height: 6' Weight: 160 Shot: Left Position: Goalie						
Sweater # 1 Years Played: 1952 - 1971						
Teams: Detroit, Chicago, St. Louis						
	GP	W	L	T	AVG	SO
	906	407	327	165	2.51	84
Playoffs:	115	49	65	-	2.79	6

Above: Glenn Hall was acquired by Chicago in a trade with Detroit.

Opposite: Hall's nickname throughout his career was "Mr. Goalie."

BOBBY HULL

Anyone who remembers watching Bobby Hull play hockey can still envision the "Golden Jet" flying down the wing, his sweater rippling in the breeze while he controlled the puck with one hand and fended off an opponent with the other. Hull could do all of that because of his broad-shouldered muscular physique developed by working at his family farm in Pointe Anne, Ontario. One of the fastest skaters in the NHL, Hull's booming shot (once clocked at 118 m.p.h.) and his bull-like rushes made him hockey's greatest attraction.

The Chicago Blackhawks were a struggling organization when Hull made his first appearance in 1957-58. He scored 18 goals as a rookie but lost out on the Calder Trophy to Toronto's Frank Mahovlich. Soon Hull's standard became 50 goals. He hit the magic half century mark for the first time when he was only 23 years old in 1962. In 1965-66, Hull became the first NHL player to pass the 50-goal plateau when a he blew a shot from the blueline past New York Ranger goalie Cesare Maniago on March 12, 1966. He ended the season with 54 in total. After scoring 52 in 1966-67, Hull shattered his own record with 58 goals in 1968-69. He had one final 50 goal year in 1971-72.

Hull's scoring exploits won him the Art Ross Trophy three times in his career. He made the first all-star team on ten different occasions. As might be expected, Hull's abilities gained him a great deal of respect from the other teams who usually had a full-time checker on him. He was clutched, grabbed and throttled by the likes of Claude Provost, Ed Westfall and Bryan Watson. However, Hull played through it all and even won the Lady Byng in 1965.

Playing for Chicago's Stanley Cup team in 1961, Hull could easily be considered the man who saved the Blackhawks' franchise. Always patient with the fans, Hull was the NHL's greatest star in his era and was a magnificent ambassador for the game.

		Born: 1-3-1939, Pointe Anne, Ontario			
Height: 5'10" Weight: 193 Shot: Left Position: Left Wing					
Sweater # 9 Years Played: 1957 - 1980					
Teams: Chicago, Winnipeg, Hartford					
	GP	G	A	PTS	PM
	1063	610	560	1170	640
Playoffs:	116	62	67	129	102

Opposite: Early in his career Hull wore number 16.

Above: Bobby Hull looks for a rebound against Leafs' Johnny Bower.

STAN MIKITA

Stan Mikita was born in Sokolce, Czechoslovakia under the name Stanislaus Gvoth. His aunt and uncle, Ann and Joe Mikita offered to take Stan back with them to Canada during a visit one year. They wanted to give the young boy a chance at a better life. Realizing the uncertainties of life in post World War II Europe, Stan's mother agreed to this adoption. Although he did not want to go, the youngster soon found himself on his way to St. Catharines, Ontario. Stan took the Mikita surname as his own and learned to live in Canada. He soon became determined to beat Canadians at their own game of hockey.

The other kids made fun of Mikita as he tried to learn English but he found a way to compete with his peers by playing hockey. Eventually, Mikita made the junior St. Catharines Teepees who were a part of the Chicago system. His goal scoring and point totals began to mount, and in 1958-59 he won the OHA scoring title with 38 goals and 59 assists. He also played in three games for Chicago in the same season, and in the following year became a permanent member of the Blackhawks.

Early in his career Mikita played with a chip on

his shoulder, spending quite a bit of time in the penalty box by taking too many misconducts. But he could also play the game. A polished skater with excellent face-off skills, Mikita was both a superb passer and checker. He was valuable at both ends of the ice.

As late as the 1964-65 season, Mikita had recorded 154 penalty minutes. By 1966-67, he came to the realization that he would be more valuable outside the penalty box, and had the best season of his career with 35 goals and 97 points. Mikita also

Born: 5-20-1940, Skolce, Czechoslovakia
Height: 5'9" Weight: 169 Shot: Right Position: Center
Sweater# 21 Years Played: 1958 - 1980
Teams: Chicago

	GP	G	A	PTS	PM
	1394	541	926	1467	1273
Playoffs:	155	59	91	150	169

became the NHL's first triple crown winner in 1967 when he won three trophies, the Hart, the Art Ross and the Lady Byng. He repeated this feat in 1968.

Many said that Mikita played in the shadow of Bobby Hull, but his career records show he had carved out his own niche. Mikita played his entire career in Chicago and his sweater number (21) is retired.

Below: Mikita is checked by Rangers' Harry Howell.

Opposite: Stan Mikita (21) tries to skate away from Montreal's Jean Guy Talbot (17).

ERIC NESTERENKO

Eric Nesterenko started his career with the Toronto Maple Leafs when he was only 19 years old. The Leafs thought he would be a star in the NHL, especially after he scored 53 goals with the junior Toronto Marlboros in 1951-52. Toronto further hoped the big 6'2" Nesterenko would help offset Montreal's new star, Jean Beliveau. However, after three seasons in Toronto averaging only 10 goals a year, the Leafs sent Nesterenko and goalie Harry Lumley to Chicago for $40,000 in May, 1956.

At first Nesterenko refused to report to Chicago and decided to retire at 23. He intended to pursue a university degree. However, Tommy Ivan of the Blackhawks was persistent and worked out a deal whereby Nesterenko could go to school during the week and play for Chicago on the weekends. He played in only 24 games for Chicago in 1956-57, scoring eight goals and finishing with 23 points. It convinced Nesterenko that he should return to hockey on a full-time basis.

His career with Chicago proved to be a long one which did not end until 1972. In his first full year with Chicago, 1957-58, Nesterenko scored a career high 20 goals. He would never score more than 20 in a single year again as he dedicated himself to being a checker with the Blackhawks. He forged out a reputation as a shadow, hounding the better scorers in the league like Gordie Howe, Johnny

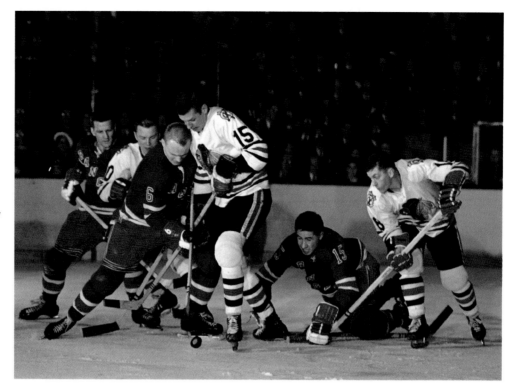

Below: Eric Nesterenko moves in for a shot against Toronto's Terry Sawchuk.

Right: Nesterenko (15) fights for the puck against the New York Rangers with help from teammate Chico Maki.

Bucyk and Frank Mahovlich. Nesterenko accepted the thankless job without complaint and became quite proficient at this line of work. He played aggressively in the early years of his career, in many seasons getting over 100 minutes in penalties. His long reach helped him to check and his use of the elbows kept the opposition on alert.

A member of the Blackhawks 1961 Stanley Cup championship, he contributed two goals and three assists in the playoff run. Even though he was not a high scorer, his career total was a very respectable 250 goals.

Born: 10-31-1933, Flin Flin, Manitoba
Height: 6'2" Weight: 197 Shot: Right Position: Right Wing
Sweater # 15   Years Played: 1951 - 1972
Teams: Toronto, Chicago, Los Angeles

	GP	G	A	PTS	PM
	1219	250	324	574	1273
Playoffs:	124	13	24	37	127

PIERRE PILOTE

Pierre Pilote grew up in the Chicago organization and it took him a while to get to the top of the ladder. Once he finished his junior career in St. Catharines, Pilote was assigned to the Buffalo Bisons of the AHL. It was difficult to break into the NHL directly from junior in those days. Pilote was green and he knew he had some learning to do. When he completed nearly four years in Buffalo, Pilote and the Blackhawks felt he was ready for the big league.

The defenseman played only 20 games for Chicago in 1955-56, but then completed a full season in 1956-57, scoring three goals and 14 assists. Pilote started to pile up the assists as his finesse game improved. He quickly became one of the league's better playmakers from the blueline. In 1963-64, Pilote's 46 assist total tied an NHL record. His best offensive year was in 1964-65 when he scored a career high 14 goals and 59 points. This mark surpassed the previous record for defensemen set by Toronto's Babe Pratt in 1943-44 when he had 57. The year the Blackhawks won the Cup in 1961, Pilote had 15 points in 12 playoff games.

On the small side for a defenseman, Pilote nonetheless played a very aggressive game. He led the NHL with 165 penalty minutes in 1960-61. His penalty minute total was usually around the 100 mark on a consistent basis. His all-round play earned

him the Norris Trophy three years in a row between 1963 and 1965. He was named to the first all-star team five consecutive years ending in 1967.

Pilote was also a very capable leader which made him a natural choice to be captain when Ed Litzenberger was traded away, and held that honour for the Blackhawks between 1961 and 1968. He was traded to Toronto for the 1968-69 season which was his last in the NHL. His great career and achievements were recognized in 1975 when he was elected to the Hockey Hall of Fame.

Born: 12-11-1931, Kenogami, Quebec				
Height: 5'10" Weight: 178 Shot: Left Position: Defense				
Sweater # 3 Years Played: 1955 - 1969				
Teams: Chicago, Toronto				
GP	G	A	PTS	PM
890	80	418	498	1251
Playoffs: 86	8	53	61	102

Above: A good offensive defenseman, Pierre Pilote (3) puts one past New York goalie Eddie Giacomin.

Opposite: Pilote checks Detroit's Andy Bathgate (21).

ELMER VASKO

Quebec native Elmer Vasko wasn't interested in hockey until his family moved to St. Catharines, Ontario. Once he started playing, a coach took one look at his size and told him he should think about playing defense. It turned out to be good advice as Vasko grew to 6'3" tall and 220 pounds. It was his size and strength that made him a force in the NHL.

Vasko played in St. Catherines for the junior Teepees in the Chicago organization. His coach in St. Catharines was Rudy Pilous who would later see Vasko in Chicago when he took over behind the Chicago bench in 1957. Vasko signed his first pro

contract with Chicago in March, 1956 after a minor league career that lasted only seven games with Buffalo of the AHL.

Another talented defenseman named Pierre Pilote also played his first full year with Chicago in 1956-57. Vasko would serve as Pilote's partner for many years and their skills complemented one another. Both players could rush the puck and each was aggressive. Vasko could really charge up the Chicago crowd with his rushes down the ice. The crowd would yell "Moooose" as the fast, but some- what ungraceful skater, charged up the rink. The nickname "Moose" stuck and it seemed to fit the rather large Vasko well. "Moose" was at his rambunctious best when he piled up 110 penalty minutes in 1959-60.

As the Blackhawks became a better team, their players gained more recognition around the league. Vasko got his share of the limelight with two consecutive second team all-star berths in 1963 and 1964. He was a member of Chicago's Stanley Cup team in 1961 when he led all players in the playoffs with 23 penalty minutes.

Vasko retired for the 1966-67 season but returned to play in Minnesota for two years. The North Stars named him captain for the 1968-69 season which was his last full year in the league.

	Born: 12-11-1935, Duparquet, Quebec				
	Height: 6'3" Weight: 220 Shot: Left Position: Defense				
	Sweater # 4 Years Played 1956 - 1970				
	Teams: Chicago, Minnesota				
	GP	G	A	PTS	PM
	786	34	166	200	719
Playoffs:	78	2	7	9	73

Below: Elmer Vasko (4) battles Detroit's Norm Ullman for the puck with teammate Jack Evans (5).

Opposite: Goalie Glenn Hall watches as Vasko moves to clear the puck away.

KEN WHARRAM

Ken Wharram played 29 games in his first season with the Chicago Blackhawks in 1953-54. However, Chicago sent him to the minors the next year and Wharram thought he would be there for a long time. As he grew accustomed to playing in the minors, Wharram found he could score goals with some consistency. Playing with the Buffalo Bisons in the AHL, Wharram posted seasons of 35, 27, 28 and 31 goals. Still, it looked as though he might never make it to the NHL.

In 1957, Buffalo coach Harry Watson shifted Wharram from center to right wing where his small build would be less of a hindrance. It proved to be a smart move when Wharram got a second chance

with the rebuilding Blackhawks in 1958-59. He played in 66 games and scored 10 goals. Eventually he was put on a line with Stan Mikita and Ab McDonald and they formed the "Scooter Line" (McDonald was later replaced by Doug Mohns). In 1963-64, Wharram made his mark in the NHL with 39 goals and 32 assists. He also won the Lady Byng Trophy. In 1966-67, when Chicago finished first, Wharram had 31 goals and had become a steady goal scorer at the NHL level.

Wharram was a fast skater who could break quickly across the opposition blueline. He was slight at 5'9" and 165 pounds, but his compact build helped him to get his body behind a quick wrist

shot. He was on the wing when the Blackhawks won the Stanley Cup in 1961, scoring 16 goals and 45 points in the season and adding another eight points in the playoffs. The player who thought he would never get back to the NHL received the recognition due him with two first team all-star berths in 1964 and 1967.

In his last NHL season, 1968-69, Wharram scored 30 goals. He finished his career with 252 career goals, all with Chicago.

		Born: 7-2-1933, Ferris, Ontario			
	Height: 5'9" Weight: 165 Shot: Right Position: Right Wing				
	Sweater # 17 Years Played: 1951 - 1969				
		Teams: Chicago			
	GP	G	A	PTS	PM
	766	252	281	533	227
Playoffs:	80	16	27	43	38

Opposite: Ken Wharram (17) scores on Toronto's Johnny Bower after beating defenseman Larry Hillman (22).

Above: Wharram (17) and Stan Mikita (21) were two-thirds of the "Scooter Line."

BILL HAY

Above: Bill Hay (11) puts a shot off the post behind Detroit's Terry Sawchuk.

Center Bill Hay was unique during his days as a hockey player. He was one of the very first to combine education with hockey when he played at Colorado College in the United States. He graduated with a degree in geology. Not many could match his credentials at his first professional training camp with the Montreal Canadiens.

The Chicago Blackhawks purchased his playing rights from the Canadiens for $25,000 after he had played for one season in Calgary of the WHL. He made Chicago's team in 1959-60 scoring 18 goals and 37 assists to capture rookie of the year honours and the Calder Trophy. Hay was teamed with Bobby Hull and Murray Balfour to form what became known as the "Million Dollar Line." The nickname for the trio came from coach Rudy Pilous who once said he wouldn't trade the three players for a million dollars. As the unit began to click, the goals started going into the net. One year they scored 50 goals in the Blackhawks last 50 games. By 1960-61 they combined for 63 goals in the 66 games they played together. It was an ideal line because it featured a playmaker, a scorer and a checker.

The 1966-67 season was Hay's last in the NHL and it saw the Blackhawks finish on top in the regular season for the first time ever. At the age of 32, Hay decided that it was a good time to put his education to use in the business world.

Born: 12-8-1935, Saskatoon, Saskatchewan
Height: 6'3" Weight: 197 Shot: Left Position: Center
Sweater # 11 Years Played: 1959 - 1967
Teams: Chicago

	GP	G	A	PTS	PM
	506	113	273	386	265
Playoffs:	67	15	21	36	62

AB McDONALD

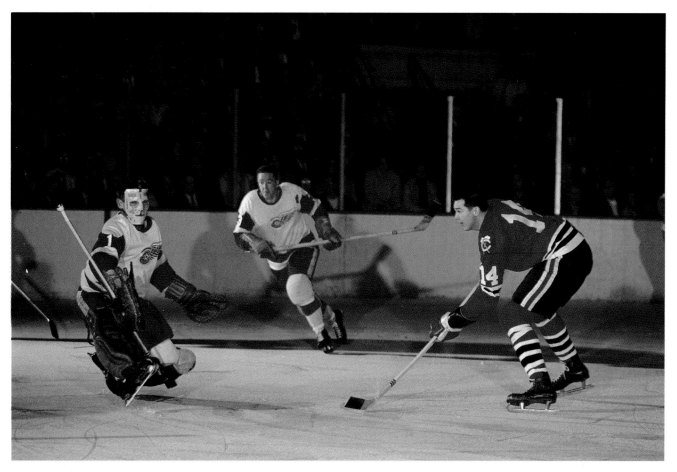

Above: Ab McDonald (14) tries to fire one behind Red Wings' goalie Terry Sawchuk.

Ab McDonald's pro career began with Rochester of the AHL in 1958, and later that year joined the Montreal during the playoffs as they won the Cup for a third straight year. He played his first full NHL season in 1958-59 contributing to the Canadiens fourth consecutive title. He had a good year scoring 13 goals and 23 assists as a rookie while playing in 69 games, but the Canadiens decided to trade McDonald to Chicago during the 1960 season.

It was easy to see why a surging Blackhawk team would be interested in the 6'2" left winger who had a good eye for the net. McDonald's low, quick and accurate wrist shots helped him put a few in the cage. His goal total with Chicago rose to 17, followed by seasons of 22 and 20 respectively. Noted for his positional play, McDonald's size allowed him to handle the heavy going. His best point total was 61 in 1962-63.

In Chicago, he became part of the "Scooter Line" with Stan Mikita and Ken Wharram. They were put together in training camp to start the 1960-61 season which culminated in the Blackhawks winning the Stanley Cup. McDonald scored the Stanley Cup winning goal against Detroit.

Born: 2-18-1936, Winnipeg, Manitoba
Height: 6'2' Weight: 194 Shot: Left Position: Left Wing
Sweater # 14   Years Played: 1957 - 1972
Teams: Montreal, Chicago, Boston
Detroit, Pittsburgh, St. Louis

	GP	G	A	PTS	PM
	762	182	248	430	200
Playoffs:	84	21	29	50	42

DETROIT RED WINGS

During the late Forties and early Fifties, the Detroit Red Wings were a dominate team in the NHL. Between 1948-49 and 1954-55, they finished first seven seasons in a row and were back on top for an eighth time in 1956-57. Twice the Red Wings recorded over 100 points in a season and four times they captured the Stanley Cup between 1950 and 1955. Their win in 1950 came in dramatic style as winger Pete Babando scored in overtime of the seventh game to beat the New York Rangers in the Finals.

The great Detroit teams were put together by Jack Adams who served as general manager of the club between 1927 and 1963. Able to spot and develop good talent, Adams had some of hockey's greatest talent assembled on one team. The fantastic "Production Line" of Gordie Howe, Sid Abel and Ted Lindsay served as the backbone of the team. Other top players included goalie Terry Sawchuk, defensemen Red Kelly, Leo Reise and Marcel Pronovost and forwards Alex Delvecchio and Tony Leswick.

Howe became a Detroit icon wearing the Red Wing sweater for 25 years. He joined the Red Wings in 1946-47 and stayed until 1970-71 scoring 786 career goals for Detroit. The six-time Hart Trophy winner will never have his longevity records matched. The Howe name has become synonymous with the Motor City. He was one of the few constants for a Detroit team that often changed players and coaches.

Saying that he didn't want complacency to set in, Adams started to trade away some of his championship players after the 1955 Stanley Cup win. A total of seven players were dealt from the Red Wings including goalie Terry Sawchuk. It was Sawchuk who led Detroit to a Stanley Cup sweep in 1952. In the Finals against Montreal, Sawchuk gave up a total of two goals in four games. He also backstopped the Red Wings in 1954 and 1955 when Detroit won two seven game series against the Canadiens in the Finals. Yet Sawchuk was gone to Boston, making room on the team for Glenn Hall.

Right: The legendary Terry Sawchuk gets assistance from Bill Gadsby.

Eventually, Adams reversed his thoughts and reaquired Sawchuk, dealing Hall to Chicago. But the Red Wings were never the same.

Adams' dismantling of the Red Wings was complete when he feuded with superstar defensemen Red Kelly. Adams believed Kelly was finished and tried to trade him to New York. He refused to report to the Rangers, deciding to retire. But the Toronto Maple Leafs struck a deal with Kelly and Adams took Marc Reaume in return. Kelly helped Toronto to four Stanley Cups while Reaume had no impact on the Red Wings. It was rather strange treatment for an eight time all-star defenseman who was the first winner of the Norris Trophy. Although the Red Wings made the Finals once more in 1956, they missed the playoffs in 1958-59 for the first time in 20 years.

While Howe, Delvecchio and Pronovost provided Detroit with long term stability, the Red Wings were able to add new people to get them back into contention. Norm Ullman joined the team in 1955-56 and became a steady performer for the Red Wings until 1968. He led the NHL in goals scored with 42 in the 1964-65 season. Some good deals brought players such as Roger Crozier, Bill Gadsby, Doug Barkley, Al Langlois, Gary Bergman and Leo Boivin. Forwards traded for included Parker MacDonald, Floyd Smith, Dean Prentice, Bryan Watson and Andy Bathgate.

The Red Wing farm system also produced some good young players like Larry Jeffrey, Pit Martin, Bruce MacGregor and Paul Henderson. The young-sters mixed well with the Detroit veterans to give them a combination which seemed to find its stride at playoff time. Sid Abel was brought in to coach and later take over from Adams in management.

In the early Sixties Detroit showed an ability to win in the playoffs, but they always came up short of the ultimate prize. They made it to the Finals in 1961 by taking out Toronto in five games, but then lost to a powerful Chicago Blackhawk team. They missed the playoffs in 1961-62, but came back to play Toronto in the Finals in 1963 and 1964 despite their unspectacular fourth place finishes both years. In 1964, the Red Wings appeared to have the Cup locked up after taking a 3 - 2 series lead in Toronto. They then lost a 4 - 3 heartbreaker in the sixth game on Bobby Baun's famous overtime goal on a broken leg. Two nights later, Toronto finished off the series with a 4 - 0 win in game seven.

The Red Wings turned in a first place finish in 1964-65 but this time were upset by the Chicago Blackhawks. In 1965-66, Detroit finished fourth place, but once again made it to the Finals. This time they lost not only the series to the Montreal Canadiens, but also the last great opportunity for some of their veterans to win a Stanley Cup.

Detroit's decline began after their loss to Montreal in 1966. The defense crumbled as Marcel Pronovost, Doug Barkley, Bill Gadsby and Terry Sawchuk all left the team in some fashion between 1965 and 1966. With no blueline to build around, the Red Wings began a period of decline that would never return them to their glory days of the 1950s.

Opposite: Detroit's two greatest stars, Gordie Howe (9) and Terry Sawchuk (1) discuss strategy.

ALEX DELVECCHIO

A former great Detroit star, Larry Aurie, had much to do with the development of a future Red Wing great, Alex Delvecchio. Aurie, a one time right winger who had his sweater number retired by the Detroit club, coached a young Delvecchio in Fort William, Ontario. Under the tutelage of Aurie, Delvecchio practiced and learned the finer points of the game.

Delvecchio moved to Oshawa where he played junior with the Generals. He led the OHA in assists with 72 in 1950-51. He started the next season with Indianapolis of the AHL and played in only six games before getting the call to Detroit. As a rookie, he played in 65 games scoring 15 goals to go along with 22 assists. In the playoffs, he added three assists in eight games in Detroit's sweep to the Stanley Cup. Detroit added a second Stanley Cup in 1953-54, and then again in 1954-55. During the 1955 playoffs, Delvecchio totalled seven goals and eight assists in 11 games. He scored twice in game seven of the Finals, leading Detroit to a 3-1 victory over the Montreal Canadiens.

A center for most of his career, Delvecchio could also play on left wing. He was named to the second all-star team at each position. During his career, Delvecchio won the Lady Byng Trophy three times, the last in 1968-69 when he recorded a personal best 83 points. A great passer, Delvecchio teamed beautifully with Gordie Howe.

Named captain in 1962, he kept the leadership role until 1974 when he retired after 24 NHL seasons. Delvecchio later served the Red Wings as a general manager and as a coach. To honour his great career, Detroit retired Delvecchio's sweater number 10 just as they did with his mentor Aurie's number 6.

Born: 12-4-1931, Fort William, Ontario					
Height: 6' Weight: 195 Shot: Left Position: Center					
Sweater # 10 Years Played: 1950 - 1974					
Teams: Detroit					
	GP	G	A	PTS	PM
	1549	456	825	1281	383
Playoffs:	121	35	69	104	29

Above: Alex Delvecchio (10) checks Chicago's Al MacNeil.

Opposite: Delvecchio gets away from Toronto's Tim Horton.

BILL GADSBY

Bill Gadsby's long career in the NHL lasted 20 years, but he almost missed the opportunity to ever start. He was nearly killed at the age of 12 when an oceanliner he was on was torpedoed in 1939. He and his mother were on the last steamship to leave England (where they were visiting family) prior to the outbreak of World War II. They were in a lifeboat for five hours in the Atlantic before being rescued.

Former NHL goalie Tiny Thompson scouted defenseman Gadsby and gave him $7,500 to turn professional with Chicago when he was 18 years old. He joined the Blackhawks during the 1946-47 season, and stayed with Chicago for eight seasons until he was dealt to New York. His best year with Chicago was in 1953-54 when he scored 12 goals and 29 assists. This came after he learned in 1952 that he had polio. It was a battle Gadsby won.

A little deceiving to the opposition since he moved slowly, Gadsby was nonetheless a punishing bodychecker. He was not afraid to take on all the tough customers including Toronto's "Bashing" Bill Barilko, perhaps the league's best hitter at the time. In a game at the Chicago Stadium, Gadsby met Barilko at centre ice. The Leaf defenseman had to crawl off the ice while Gadsby hurt his shoulder. Such was the nature of a Gadsby hit.

He may have been tough but he could also rush the puck and make passes with authority. He had a heavy, accurate shot which made him valuable on the point during the power play. In 1958-59, while with the Rangers, he set a new mark for defensemen with 46 assists making him the first to break Doug Harvey's mark of 44. He made the first all-star team three times in his career.

Traded to Detroit in 1961, the Red Wings made the Finals three times before Gadsby retired but a Stanley Cup victory still proved to be elusive.

		Born: 8-8-1927, Calgary, Alberta			
Height: 6'	Weight: 185	Shot: Left	Position: Defense		
	Sweater # 4	Years Played: 1946 - 1966			
	Teams: Chicago, New York Rangers, Detroit				
GP	G	A	PTS	PM	
1248	130	437	567	1539	
67	4	23	27	92	

Above: Bill Gadsby (4) watches Gordie Howe take the puck away for a charge up the ice.

Opposite: Gadsby tries to get good position on Montreal's Gilles Tremblay.

GORDIE HOWE

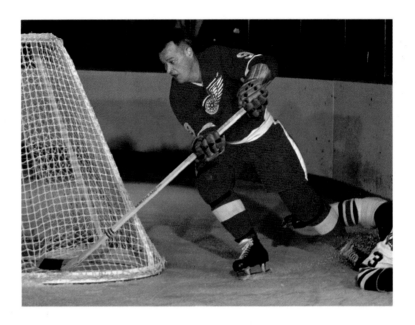

Gordie Howe's title of "Mister Hockey" was earned after 32 years of playing the game at the professional level. Considering the length of his career, it's easy to make a case for calling Howe the greatest player of all-time. Many of his longevity records are not likely to be challenged in the future. Howe's career began in 1946 and did not finish until 1980 — playing in five decades!

At the age of 15, Howe attended a New York Rangers tryout camp. The native of Floral, Saskatchewan felt homesick so he left, but the next year he went to the Detroit Red Wings' camp in Windsor, Ontario. Detroit manager Jack Adams signed Howe to his first pro contract in 1945 when he turned 17. He was assigned to Omaha of the USHL and scored 22 goals and 26 assists in 51 games. He never played in the minors again. By 1946-47, Howe was a regular with the Detroit team and was earning $2,600 a year.

Howe scored a goal in his first NHL game against Toronto's Turk Broda, but only had a total of seven as a rookie. When he teamed with Sid Abel and Ted Lindsay to form the fabled "Production Line", Howe started to pour goals past opposing netminders. He finished his NHL career with 801 goals. He won six scoring titles and the same number of Hart Trophies as the league's best player. He became the first player to break Maurice Richard's career record of 544 goals and was a

fixture on the NHL all-star teams from 1956 to 1970. Strong on his skates and gifted with a quick wrist shot, Howe was still producing big numbers at the age of 41 when he scored 103 points in 1968-69, his best as a Red Wing.

A physical hockey player, Howe had few who challenged him on the ice. A man of extraordinary strength and mean disposition when necessary, Howe's reputation was forever solidified when he pounded Ranger tough guy Lou Fontinato in a 1959 fight. A four time Stanley Cup winner with Detroit, Howe returned to the NHL with the Hartford Whalers in 1979-80 and played with sons Mark and Marty.

Born: 3-31-1928, Floral, Saskatchewan					
Height: 6' Weight: 205 Shot: Right Position: Right Wing					
Sweater # 9 Years Played: 1946 - 1980					
Teams: Detroit, Hartford					
	GP	G	A	PTS	PM
	1767	801	1049	1850	1685
Playoffs:	157	68	92	160	220

Opposite: Howe (9) has Rangers' goalie Gump Worsley (1) down with a good chance to score.

Above: Gordie Howe played 25 seasons for the Red Wings.

MARCEL PRONOVOST

Detroit Red Wings scout Marcel Cote was taking a close look at the Wilson brothers, Johnny and Larry. After watching a game Cote decided he had another prospect in defenseman Marcel Pronovost. It proved to be a good trip for the Detroit scout as all three players would eventually wear Red Wing uniforms in the NHL.

Growing up in Shawinigan Falls, Quebec, Pronovost wanted to play for the Montreal Canadiens. When no Montreal scout called, he signed with the Red Wings. Pronovost turned professional in the spring of 1948 and played for Omaha of the USHL in 1949-50. When Omaha was eliminated from the playoffs, Detroit called him up to the NHL for post-season action. The Red Wings knocked off Toronto and New York to win the Stanley Cup, and gave a 19 year-old Pronovost his first championship. An injury to Gordie Howe in the Toronto series forced defenseman Red Kelly to move up to forward. It created an opening at the blueline which Pronovost filled very capably.

One of the toughest players ever to play in the NHL, Pronovost's tolerance for pain was nothing short of amazing. He suffered countless injuries but always found a way to play. In the 1961 Final when Detroit met Chicago, Pronovost played four games on a badly cracked ankle. He would arrive at the rink on crutches, play the game and then put his foot back into a cast!

Pronovost was a graceful skater and proved to be a good puck carrier who had some offensive punch. His best year with Detroit saw him score 9 goals and 25 assists in 1954-55. He was named to the first and second all-star teams twice each as a Red Wing. He was traded to Toronto in May, 1965 and played a vital role in the Leafs' Stanley Cup win of 1967. It was Pronovost's fifth Stanley Cup title. He stayed with Toronto until 1970.

		Born: 6-15-1930, Lac la Tortue, Quebec			
		Height: 6' Weight: 190 Shot: Left Position: Defense			
		Sweater # 3 Years Played: 1950 -1970			
		Teams: Detroit, Toronto			
	GP	G	A	PTS	PM
	1206	88	257	345	821
Playoffs:	134	12	25	37	116

Opposite: Marcel Pronovost skates away from Boston's Dean Prentice.

Above: Pronovost played on a Stanley Cup winner as a rookie in 1950.

TERRY SAWCHUK

Any goaltender who could win the rookie of the year award in three different professional leagues had to have stardom written all over him. Such was the case for Terry Sawchuk who won his first rookie award with Omaha of the USHL when he was only 18 years old. He followed that up as the best first year player at Indianapolis of the AHL. Finally, he won the Calder Trophy with the Detroit Red Wings in 1950-51. In his first year with Detroit, Sawchuk played in all 70 games, recording 11 shut-outs and a 1.98 goals against average. He missed the Vezina Trophy by just one goal!

Sawchuk first started playing hockey as a goalie but then decided to switch to center. As a bantam aged player in Winnipeg, Sawchuk won the scoring championship which included an eight goal performance in one game. He went back to play in

the net and the Detroit Red Wings were very glad he did. A year after his great rookie season Sawchuk had an amazing performance in the 1952 playoffs when he recorded four shutouts in eight games and allowed a paultry five goals over all. Detroit swept to the Stanley Cup without a loss!

Although he helped Detroit to three Stanley Cups and was the winner of the Vezina Trophy on three occasions, Sawchuk was dealt to the Boston Bruins in 1955. He stayed there for a couple of rather unhappy seasons before Detroit reacquired him in 1957. The Red Wings made three more trips to the Finals with Sawchuk but they lost them all.

Available in the inter-league draft, Sawchuk was picked up by the Maple Leafs in June, 1964. Sawchuk shared the Vezina Trophy with the Leafs' Johnny Bower in 1964-65 and had his last great

moment with Toronto in the 1967 playoffs. He was at his best against Chicago, and then Montreal in the Cup finals when he stymied the Canadiens' attack time after time.

Using a somewhat unorthodox crouching style, Sawchuk used his big hands and quick reflexes to record 103 career shutouts. This is a record that will never be broken.

Opposite: Terry Sawchuk recorded 103 career shutouts.

Above: Bill Gadsby defends against Boston's Orland Kurtenbach (25) while Sawchuk searches for the puck.

Born: 12-28-1929, Winnipeg, Manitoba

Height: 6' Weight: 195 Shot: Left Position: Goalie

Sweater # 1 Years Played: 1949 - 1970

Teams: Detroit, Boston, Toronto, Los Angles, New York Rangers

	GP	W	L	T	AVG	SO
	971	435	337	188	2.52	103
Playoffs:	106	54	48	-	2.54	12

NORM ULLMAN

Norm Ullman was not especially colourful or flamboyant over his 20 year NHL career. A top forechecker and digger, Ullman's playmaking skills made him a consistent goal scorer and point getter. Good at shooting quickly from the slot, Ullman was also especially adroit at making pinpoint passes to his wingers. Playing in the shadow of Gordie Howe and Alex Delvecchio, Ullman was content to do his job quietly but effectively.

A star with Edmonton in junior, Ullman also played minor league hockey in the same city in the WHL. He came to Detroit in 1955-56 and two years later scored 23 goals. It marked the first of 12 consecutive seasons Ullman would pass the 20 goal plateau (in all he had 16 seasons of 20 or more

goals). His best year with Detroit was in 1964-65 when he scored 42 times to lead the NHL. His point total was just one behind Art Ross Trophy winner Stan Mikita. His performance earned him a first team all-star berth as the league's top centre for the only time in his career.

Ullman proved he could be a clutch performer in the playoffs. In the 1963 playoffs, Ullman had 16 points in 11 games and followed that with 17 points in 14 games in the 1964 post season. On April 11, 1965 Ullman set an NHL record by scoring two goals in five seconds in a playoff game against Chicago. The record has never been broken.

Despite his great performance with Detroit, he was traded to Toronto in March, 1968 along with wingers Paul Henderson and Floyd Smith in return for Frank Mahovlich, Peter Stemkowski, Garry Unger and Carl Brewer. Ullman had his best season with Toronto in 1970-71 when he scored 34 goals and 85 points. That point total stayed as a Leaf record until broken by Darryl Sittler.

Despite four trips to the Stanley Cup Finals, the championship still eluded Ullman but his great career was recognized with his election to the Hall of Fame in 1982.

Below: Norm Ullman (7) shoots the puck past Boston Goalie Eddie Johnston (1).

Opposite: Ullman led the NHL in goals scored with 42 in 1964-65.

Born: 12-26-1935, Provost, Alberta					
Height: 5'10" Weight: 175 Shot: Left Position: Left Wing					
Sweater # 7 Years Played: 1955 - 1975					
Teams: Detroit, Toronto, Edmonton					
	GP	G	A	PTS	PM
	1410	490	739	1229	712
Playoffs:	106	30	53	83	67

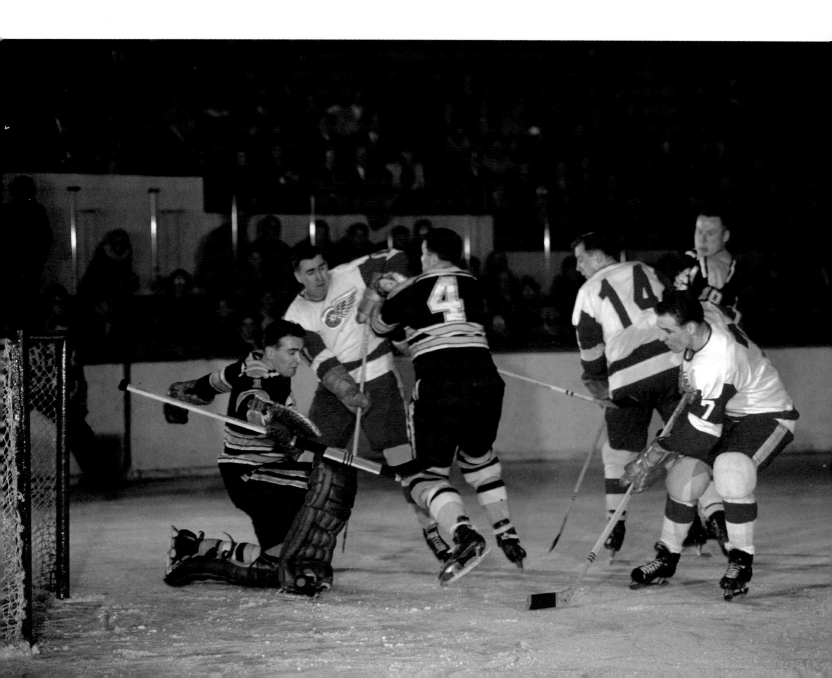

DOUG BARKLEY

Above: Doug Barkley (5) battles Toronto's Red Kelly for a loose puck.

Detroit Red Wings coach Sid Abel spotted Doug Barkley playing in the Chicago minor system, and offered the Blackhawks' Len Lunde and Johnny McKenzie for Barkley's services. They accepted and Barkley stepped right into the Red Wing lineup. Handing out some punishing bodychecks, Barkley added an aggressive element to a team that really needed some bulk. His play placed him second in the rookie of the year honours in 1962-63.

Barkley's first NHL goal came against Toronto goalie Johnny Bower in a 7-3 Detroit win. It was shot that Barkley put low into the corner of the net. Learning to keep his shot along the ice helped Barkley score 11 goals in 1964-65 to lead all defensemen in the NHL.

Just as his career was starting to blossom, it was cut short 43 games into the 1965-66 season. An errant stick caught Barkley in the eye and ended his playing days. He went to work for the Red Wings in their front office holding a variety of jobs, including coach for three seasons.

	Born: 1-6-1937, Lethbridge, Alberta				
	Height: 6'2" Weight: 185 Shot: Right Position: Defense				
	Sweater # 5 Years Played:1957 - 1966				
	Teams: Chicago, Detroit				
	GP	G	A	PTS	PM
	253	24	80	104	382
Playoffs:	30	0	9	9	63

ROGER CROZIER

Above: Roger Crozier (1) stops a shot from Toronto's Larry Jeffrey.

An opportunity developed for 22 year old Roger Crozier when the Detroit Red Wings let goaltender Terry Sawchuk go to Toronto. He made the most of his chances, winning the Calder Trophy as rookie of the year in 1964-65. His incredible start included a first team all-star selection and leading the league in shutouts with six.

Crozier's goaltending style was unorthodox to say the least. A real acrobat, Crozier was often spectacular as he sprawled to stop shots. He displayed a great glove hand which made him most effective. He followed his great rookie year with another league high seven shutouts in 1965-66.

Like many other goalies, Crozier found the pressures of the job to be unbearable at times. Plagued with medical problems including an ulcer, Crozier had to leave hockey briefly in 1967-68.

He returned to the Red Wings for two more seasons before going to the Buffalo Sabres in their first year of existence, 1970-71. He was with the Sabres when they made it to the Finals in 1975 against Philadelphia.

Born: 3-16-1942, Bracebridge, Ontario
Height: 5'8" Weight: 140 Shot: Right Position: Goaltender
Sweater #1 Years Played 1963 - 1977
Teams: Detroit, Buffalo, Washington

	GP	W	L	T	AVG	SO
	518	206	197	74	3.04	30
Playoffs:	31	14	15	-	2.78	1

PAUL HENDERSON

Above: Paul Henderson (19) uses his speed to get away from Boston's Dean Prentice (17).

Every Canadian remembers where they were when Paul Henderson scored the winning goal with only 34 seconds left in the final game of the 1972 Summit Series against the Soviet Union gaining a 6-5 win for Team Canada. Henderson's third consecutive game winning goal capped a tremendous comeback for the Canadian team who were expected to breeze past the Soviets. The speedy winger's dramatic performance in the series proved to be the highlight of his hockey career.

Henderson first came to prominence when he scored 18 goals in a juvenile game. A newspaper story about this game caught the eye of scouts with Detroit who signed the phenom to a minor league contract with Hamilton of the OHA, where he scored a league high 49 goals in 1962-63 season and help his team win the Memorial Cup in 1962.

A superb skater with blazing speed, Henderson's hard, quick and accurate shot helped him score goals on a consistent basis. He was also fortunate to spend most of his career with playmaking center Norm Ullman, first in Detroit and then Toronto where they were traded in 1968.

Born: 1-28-1943, Kincardine, Ontario					
Height: 5'11" Weight:180 Shot Right Position: Left Wing					
Sweater # 19 Years Played:1962 - 1980					
Teams: Detroit, Toronto, Atlanta					
	GP	G	A	PTS	PM
	707	236	242	478	296
Playoffs:	56	11	14	25	28

TED LINDSAY

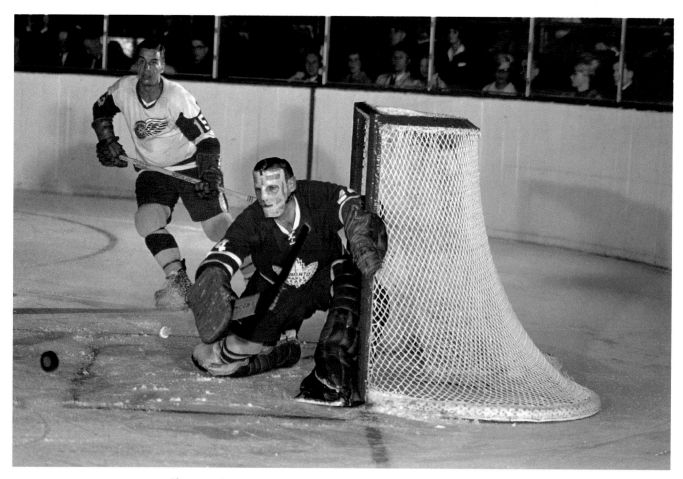

Above: Ted Lindsay waits for a rebound against Toronto's Terry Sawchuk.

Those that remember "Terrible Ted" Lindsay's bad-boy image on the ice may also remember that he played the game with a high degree of skill. He finished with 379 career goals and was on four Stanley Cup teams with Detroit. He was also named to the first all-star team as the league's best left winger a total of eight times!

Lindsay showed an ability to score goals in his first NHL season in 1944-45 when he netted 17. He was soon teamed with Gordie Howe and Sid Abel to form hockey's most feared trio, "The Production Line". In 1949-50 Lindsay won the Art Ross Trophy, leading the league in points and assists.

Lindsay had a reputation as one of the toughest customers in the NHL, and he staged some epic battles with hardrocks like Fern Flaman, Jim Thomson, Dickie Moore and Bill Ezinicke. By the time his career was over, Lindsay had become the NHL all-time penalty minute leader.

He ended his career as coach and general manager of Detroit between 1977 and 1981. His sweater number (7) is now retired by the Red Wings and he was named to the Hall of Fame in 1966.

Born: 7-29-1925, Renfrew, Ontario					
Height: 5'8" Weight: 160 Shot: Left Position: Left Wing					
Sweater Number: 7 Years Played: 1944 to 1965					
Teams: Detroit, Chicago					
	GP	G	A	Pts	PM
	1068	379	472	851	1808
Playoffs:	133	47	49	96	194

MONTREAL CANADIENS

When Frank Selke Sr. was named general manager of the Montreal Canadiens in 1946, he took over a team that had won two Stanley Cups in the three previous seasons.In the ten years before that, the Canadiens had been shut out of the Stanley Cup between 1932 and 1942. In the early Forties, the Canadiens' franchise was in trouble as attendance dwindled in what was then a rather unattractive Montreal Forum. Selke, who learned his trade in Toronto under Conn Smythe, knew he had to keep the team winning if it was to survive. There was some rebuilding to do, but the Canadiens did have the best player in hockey, Maurice "the Rocket" Richard.

Under the coaching of Dick Irvin, the Canadiens captured three Stanley Cups and made the Finals on four other occasions including Irvin's last season in 1954-55. Selke chose Toe Blake to replace the highly successful Irvin. Blake proved to be an excellent choice winning the Stanley Cup his first five seasons between 1956 and 1960. A determined, intense and fiery coach, Blake kept his players focused and got the most out of a very talented group of players.

The team that won five consecutive Stanley Cups was largely built through the Montreal farm system. This included the development of players like Bernie Geoffrion, Dickie Moore, Henri Richard, Tom Johnson, Claude Provost and Dollard St. Laurent. They joined players like Jacques Plante, Doug Harvey and Maurice Richard. In addition, the Canadiens went out and signed Jean Beliveau. By 1960, the Canadiens won the Stanley Cup in eight games straight and had won 40 of 44 playoff contests to that point. Montreal was the first team to win five Stanley Cups in a row and their championship teams of 1959 and 1960 are considered two of the best in NHL history.

The Canadiens liked to play an attacking style that became known as "fire wagon hockey." Always great skaters, the Canadiens dominated with goals. They were so efficient on the power play that the NHL changed the rules to allow a penalized player to come out

Right: The great Jacques Plante robs Chicago's Ron Murphy, as defenseman Tom Johnson looks on.

of the penalty box if a goal was scored. Their greatest goal scorer was Maurice Richard who had 544 career goals and another 82 in the playoffs. The first player to score 50 goals in a season, Richard was the inspirational leader of the Canadiens and a symbol of their glory years between 1955 and 1960. Rocket Richard was the embodiment of the Canadiens' style of play.

The Canadiens may have had more accent on the attack but they also had a great goalie in Jacques Plante.He won six Vezina Trophies and was also the last netminder to win the Hart as the NHL's best player in 1962. A great deal of the Montreal attack was generated by seven-time Norris Trophy winner Doug Harvey.He acted as a quarterback for forwards Beliveau, Richard, Moore and Bert Olmstead.Jean Guy Talbot, Bob Turner and Al Langlois were good defensemen who ensured that the Canadiens powerhouse had no weak spots. In addition to the five consecutive Cup wins, the Canadiens finished first six years out of seven between 1956 and 1962.

After the 1960 Stanley Cup win, the Rocket retired and the Canadiens began a slight decline. Some of the older stars had to be replaced with new players and it took a little bit of time until they put it all together. Although there were no Stanley Cups between 1961 and 1964, the Canadiens were soon replenished with players like J.C. Tremblay, Jacques Laperriere, Gilles Tremblay, Charlie Hodge, Ralph Backstrom, Bobby Rousseau, Ted Harris and Terry Harper.It was this group that would mix with veterans Beliveau, Provost and Henri Richard.

Many of the new players were recruited and developed by Sam Pollock who was named to replace Selke in 1964. Pollock had risen through the organization by first coaching the Montreal Junior Canadiens to a Memorial Cup and then serving as general manager of the Hull-Ottawa team in the EPHL. Pollock was later named the Canadiens director of player personnel and finally as the general manager. He would guide the Canadiens until 1978, winning nine Stanley Cups in the process.

Pollock's rise to the top job in Montreal was typical of the Canadiens organization. Good management and coaching instilled in their players a temperament that would not tolerate losing. The Canadiens learned to dig deep for that little extra, especially in the playoffs when all is on the line.

In the 1965 post season, the Canadiens regained the Stanley Cup by first knocking off defending champion Toronto in six games and then disposing of Chicago in seven. The seventh game against the Blackhawks was played in the Forum. The Canadiens were hungry for the title and they stormed the Chicago net with Jean Beliveau scoring after just 14 seconds. Montreal won the game 4 - 0 behind the shutout netminding of Gump Worsley who the Canadiens had rescued from New York.

In 1966, the Canadiens repeated as champions. The Detroit Red Wings won the first two games of the Finals in Montreal, but the Canadiens went to Detroit and swept the next two games . A 5 - 1 romp at home was followed by a 3 - 2 overtime win

Below: Jean Beliveau (4) moves in alone on Toronto's Johnny Bower (1).

Opposite: Montreal coach Toe Blake holds court with his players.

the sixth game back in Detroit. It was a controversial winner as Henri Richard slid into the RedWings goal and somehow the puck got past Roger Crozier. Detroit protested but the goal stood.

After losing the Stanley Cup to Toronto in 1967, they rebounded to win two straight titles with new stars like Yvan Cournoyer, John Ferguson, Serge Savard, Jacques Lemaire and Rogie Vachon. They started the decade of the Seventies in typical fashion by winning a surprise Stanley Cup in 1971.

Over the years the players and managers have changed but the winning has continued for the Canadiens. They spend money as needed and emphasize talent and planning. They are well aware there is a tradition to uphold. The players are reminded of this every day when they walk into the dressing room and read the passage from the poem "In Flanders Fields" which is placed on the wall.

"To you from failing hands we throw the torch,
Be yours to hold it high."

JEAN BELIVEAU

Jean Beliveau's signature on a contract with the Montreal Canadiens to start the 1953-54 season was met with considerable fanfare. He was already a legend in Quebec City where he had played junior and senior hockey. He was treated so well there, Beliveau found it hard to leave for the bright lights of Montreal. However, by the age of 22, Beliveau knew he had to pursue his dream of playing for the Canadiens. The Montreal club knew what it was getting after having Beliveau up for a trial (5 goals in 3 games) but were not quite sure they could pry him away. Finally, they decided to open the vault and let him take what he wanted.

The big centerman proved he was worth the fuss as he lived up to all expectations. Taking the role of representing French Canada very seriously, Beliveau played with poise and intelligence on the ice and had a quiet dignity about him off the ice. He quickly filled the void left by the retirement of Maurice Richard as leader of the Canadiens and hero to the province of Quebec. With Big Jean in charge, the only goal the Canadiens had in mind was winning the Stanley Cup every year.

Starting with the string of five wins in a row in 1956, Beliveau was on ten Stanley Cup winning teams. His last five Cup victories (between 1965 and 1971) were with teams he captained and had been completely overhauled. Beliveau's hockey skills

included a combination of size, strength, agility and the aggressiveness needed to play a physical game. He twice led the league in goals scored and captured the Hart Trophy on two occasions as well. For his play in the 1965 playoffs, Beliveau was named the first winner of the Conn Smythe Trophy. He also scored the winning goal in the seventh game of the Finals against Chicago.

Admired by teammates and opponents alike, Beliveau left the game after the Canadiens' Stanley Cup win in 1971. Beliveau ended his career in a classy manner befitting a man who served as a role model for so many people.

	Born: 8-31-1931, Trois Rivieres, Quebec				
	Height: 6'3" Weight: 205 Shot: Left Position: Center				
	Sweater # 4 Years Played: 1950 - 1971				
	Teams: Montreal				
	GP	G	A	PTS	PM
	1125	507	712	1219	1029
Playoffs:	162	79	97	176	211

Opposite: Jean Beliveau tries to find the puck against Toronto's Johnny Bower (1) and Tim Horton (7)

Above: Beliveau took over the Montreal captaincy when Maurice Richard retired.

BERNIE GEOFFRION

As a youngster Bernie Geoffrion liked to practice his hard slapshot. The sound of the puck hitting the boards with a thundering echo gave rise to Geoffrion's nickname "Boom Boom." Later, it provided the image Montreal broadcasting legend Danny Gallivan used for the phrase "a cannonading shot." Geoffrion used his powerful shot to become a feared shooter during his entire hockey career.

Geoffrion's scoring prowess was evident in juniors when he scored 103 goals in just 57 games. He kept on scoring as a rookie in the NHL when he fired in 30 goals for the Montreal Canadiens during 1951-52. This performance won Geoffrion the Calder Trophy as top rookie. In 1954-55, Geoffrion won his first Art Ross Trophy as he led the NHL in goals (38)

and points (75). The 1960-61 season saw Geoffrion win his second scoring championship with 95 points. He scored 50 goals that year, becoming only the second man in NHL history to do so. On March 16, 1961 Geoffrion scored against Toronto goalie Cesare Maniago thus matching the standard set by former teammate Rocket Richard.

A determined player who enjoyed a wide open game, Geoffrion played on six Stanley Cup teams in his career with Montreal. In the 1961 playoffs as the

Opposite: Bernie Geoffrion moves around the Chicago net for a shot against Chicago's Denis DeJordy.

Above: Geoffrion was the second player in NHL history to score 50 goals in one season.

Canadiens tried to win their sixth consecutive Cup, Geoffrion removed a cast from his injured knee to play a game against the Blackhawks. It was an effort that spoke clearly about Geoffrion's desire to win. It did not, however, help Montreal overcome Chicago, thus ending the great dynasty.

Geoffrion left the game in 1964 as the Canadiens went with younger players. In 1966-67, the New York Rangers talked Geoffrion out of retirement. He responded with 17 goals and 25 assists while taking a regular shift.

Born: 2-16-1931, Montreal, Quebec
Height: 5'11"   Weight: 185   Shot: Right   Position: Right Wing
Sweater # 5   Years Played: 1950 - 1968
Teams: Montreal, New York

	GP	G	A	PTS	PM
	883	393	429	822	689
Playoffs:	132	58	60	118	88

JACQUES LAPERRIERE

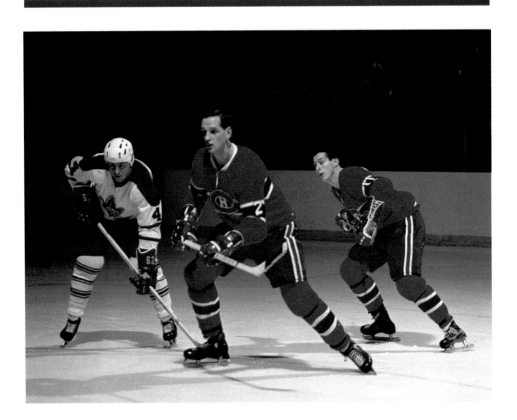

Maybe it was because he wore the number (2) on his back like his idol that Jacques Laperriere was compared to Doug Harvey. Laperriere watched the Canadiens on television as he grew up and there was no doubt Harvey was his favourite. Laperriere could not have picked a better player to emulate as he rose in the Canadiens system.

At 14 years of age, Laperriere played for the Canadiens midget team in Noranda, Quebec. By 16 he was playing junior hockey with the Hull-Ottawa Canadiens of the EPHL, he made it to Montreal as a 21 year-old. As a rookie, Laperriere played in 64 games, scoring twice and adding 28 assists while accumulating 102 penalty minutes. It earned him the Calder Trophy as the NHL's top rookie and a berth on the second all-star team. In his second season, Laperriere made the first all-star team and won the Norris Trophy as the league's best defenseman, in spite of the fact that he missed some games and the entire playoffs with an injury.

Tall (6'2") and lanky, Laperriere used his long reach with great effectiveness to poke his stick at the opponent who was about to shoot. He would either knock the puck away or deflect it into the crowd behind the Canadiens' net. Although he wasn't a smooth skater, Laperriere was a straight ahead rusher when he got control of the puck.

Laperriere played his entire career in Montreal where he was part of six Stanley Cup wins. He has served as a long-time assistant coach with the Canadiens. He had that role when Montreal won the Stanley Cup in 1986.

		Born: 11-22-1941, Rouyn, Quebec			
	Height: 6'2" Weight: 190 Shot: Left Position: Defense				
	Sweater # 2 Years Played: 1962 - 1974				
	Teams: Montreal				
	GP	G	A	PTS	PM
	691	40	242	282	674
Playoffs:	88	9	22	31	101

Opposite: Jacques Laperriere defends against Detroit's Gordie Howe.

Above: Laperriere is ready for the face-off opposite Toronto's Red Kelly (4).

JACQUES PLANTE

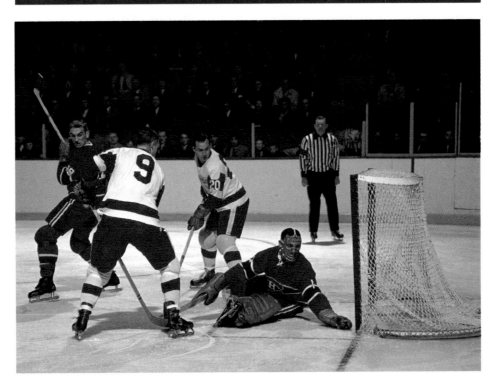

Goaltender Jacques Plante made his mark in hockey history as an innovator. His best known contribution to the game was as a result of a game on March 1, 1959 against the New York Rangers at Madison Square Garden. Rangers' Andy Bathgate ripped a backhand shot at a screened Plante who did not see the puck until it hit him smack in the face, tearing open his nose. With no backup available on the bench in those days, Plante skated off to get stitched. After repairs were completed, Plante told Montreal coach Toe Blake he would not return to the net without a face mask. The Canadiens won the game 3 - 1, went on to win their fifth consecutive Stanley Cup while Plante won the Vezina Trophy. Plante was not the first goalie to use a mask but his performance made sure that it was here to stay.

Another first from Plante was to come out of the net to handle the puck. He did this in junior hockey when he played behind a poor defense. Taking matters into his own hands, he started to clear the puck out of his end. When it proved to be effective, he kept on doing it. Plante also started the practice of raising his arm signifying an icing call to help out his defensemen.

When he wasn't busy thinking of new ideas, Plante also did a great deal of puck stopping. He was the last goalie to win the Hart Trophy for his performance in 1961-62. A major part of six Montreal Stanley Cups, Plante won the Vezina Trophy six times as well.

Montreal traded him to New York where he played for two years before retiring. He made a return to the NHL with the St. Louis Blues, sharing a Vezina Trophy with Glenn Hall. He made the second all-star team while with Toronto in 1970-71, and finished his career with the Boston Bruins.

Born: 1-17-1929, Mont Carmel, Quebec
Height: 6' Weight: 175 Shot: Left Position: Goalie
Sweater # 1   Years Played: 1952 - 1973
Teams: Montreal, New York Rangers, St. Louis, Toronto, Boston

	GP	W	L	T	AVG	SO
	837	434	246	137	2.38	82
Playoffs:	112	71	37	-	2.17	15

Opposite: Jacques Plante (1) moves to sweep the puck away.

Above: Plante goes down to try and stop Detroit's Gordie Howe (9) and Parker MacDonald (20).

CLAUDE PROVOST

For the most part, Claude Provost did the grinding work required for a successful hockey team. His main role was not to score goals but to keep the big guns on the other team silent. Since the Canadiens had so many good shooters who could provide plenty of offence, someone had to accept the unglamorous checking role. It was a job Provost did very well with a hustling and aggressive style.

His role may have been defined as defensive specialist but Provost proved he could score as well. His first NHL goal came in his rookie year, 1955-56. In the 1961-62 season, he scored 33 goals which was high on a Montreal team that included such players

as Jean Beliveau, Henri Richard and Bernie Geoffrion. In 1964-65, Provost scored 27 goals and 37 assists and was named to the first all-star team.

It took a while for Provost to receive personal recognition, but the teams he played on were always winners. Along with Beliveau and Richard, Provost was one of three players to be with the Canadiens during two winning eras. Provost was a part of the Canadiens five straight titles in the late Fifties and then was with the Habs in the Sixties when they won four Cups in five years between 1965 and 1969. Provost's top playoff performance came in 1959 when he had six goals and eight assists in 11 games. However, he was really on top of his game when he was checking the likes of Chicago's Bobby Hull with a fierce determination.

Provost's contributions to hockey were recognized toward the end of his career when he was named the first winner of the Masterton Trophy in 1968. It was a worthy award for the right winger who played 15 years in Montreal.

Below: Provost (14) attempts to score on the Leafs' Johnny Bower.

Opposite: Claude Provost scored a career high 33 goals in 1961-62.

Born: 9-17-1933, Montreal, Quebec
Height: 5'9"   Weight: 175   Shot: Right   Position: Right Wing
Sweater # 14   Years Played: 1955 - 1970
Teams: Montreal

	GP	G	A	PTS	PM
	1005	254	335	589	469
Playoffs:	126	25	38	63	86

HENRI RICHARD

As a 19 year old, Henri Richard went to his first training camp with the Montreal Canadiens in 1955 knowing he was not as good as his idol and brother Maurice. Henri decided he was going to make an impression. Displaying his great low-to-the-ice skating abilities and incredible puck control, the younger Richard made the Canadiens team.

Small at 5'7" and 165 pounds, Henri had to show that he was not afraid to take on bigger opponents. In his first year he battled tough guys like Fern Flaman, Jack Bionda, Leo Labine and Fleming MacKell, and established his reputation in the league. By his third season in the NHL, 1957-58, Richard scored 28 goals and 52 assists making the

league's first all-star team at center. His 80 points put him just four behind teammate Dickie Moore for the Art Ross Trophy. He followed this with three nominations to the second all-star team.

With the retirement of his brother Maurice, the "Pocket Rocket" emerged from the enormous shadow cast by the senior Richard. A consistent performer throughout his career, Richard also developed a reputation for scoring goals in clutch situations. In the 1966 Finals against Detroit, Richard somehow managed to get the puck past Roger Crozier in the sixth game while sprawled on the ice. The overtime win gave Montreal their second consecutive Stanley Cup. In 1971 against Chicago,

*Opposite: Always in the middle of the action,
Henri Richard battles with a group of Blackhawks.*

*Above: Richard (16) moves in to check Chicago's
Bobby Hull (16).*

Richard scored two goals, including the winner as the Canadiens won the game 3-2, and the Cup, in a thrilling seven game series.

When Jean Beliveau retired in 1971, it was Henri who was named a captain of the Canadiens. In 1973, the Habs captured the Stanley Cup and he was presented with the trophy as captain for the first time. In all, Henri Richard won the Stanley Cup an astounding 11 times in a 20 year career. It is quite likely no pro athlete will ever enjoy such success.

	Born: 2-29-1936, Montreal, Quebec				
	Height: 5'7" Weight: 160 Shot: Right Position: Center				
	Sweater # 16 Years Played: 1955 - 1975				
	Teams: Montreal				
	GP	**G**	**A**	**PTS**	**PM**
	1256	358	688	1046	928
Playoffs:	180	49	80	129	181

MAURICE RICHARD

The NHL has never seen a playoff performer like Maurice "Rocket" Richard since he retired from the Montreal Canadiens in 1960. A fierce competitor who saved his best for the post season, Richard retired with 82 career playoff goals. Included in those goals were six overtime scores, 18 game winners and seven hat tricks. It took many years before his playoff goal total was passed.

Richard's first dramatic playoff performance came on March 23, 1944 as he scored five goals in one game against the Toronto Maple Leafs. He scored all the Montreal goals in a 5 - 1 Canadiens win, despite having one of the Leafs top defensive players, Bob Davidson, assigned to check him. He was named as all three stars of the game.

The Rocket's best individual effort may have come in the seventh game of the 1952 Semi-Finals against Boston. Earlier in the game, Richard had been knocked dizzy on a hit by Leo Labine and Bill Quakenbush. He also suffered a nasty cut on his forehead. In a wobbly, if not semi-conscious state, a bloodied Richard returned to the ice late in the third period with the score tied 1-1. He took a pass in his own end, went the length of the rink before whipping a shot past goalie Jim Henry for a Canadiens victory.

Scoring goals came rather easily to Richard. He was the first player in NHL history to score 50 goals in one season. He turned the trick in 1944-45 when they only played 50 games in the regular schedule. Richard was also the first player to score 500 career goals. A great stick handler with shifty moves,

Richard's deadly shot allowed him to score from all angles. Although he never won an Art Ross Trophy, he was a first team all-star eight times.

His fiery temper would land the Rocket in trouble with the league, but there was no doubt he was the NHL's most dynamic performer and a sports legend much like Babe Ruth was in baseball.

Born: 8-4-1921, Montreal, Quebec					
Height: 5'10" Weight: 195 Shot: Left Position: Right Wing					
Sweater # 9 Years Played: 1942 - 1960					
Teams: Montreal					
	GP	G	A	PTS	PM
	978	544	421	965	1285
Playoffs:	133	82	44	126	188

95

Opposite: Maurice "the Rocket" Richard is watched by Detroit's Marcel Pronovost (3).

Below: The Richard brothers, Maurice (9) and Henri (16) apply pressure on the Leaf's net.

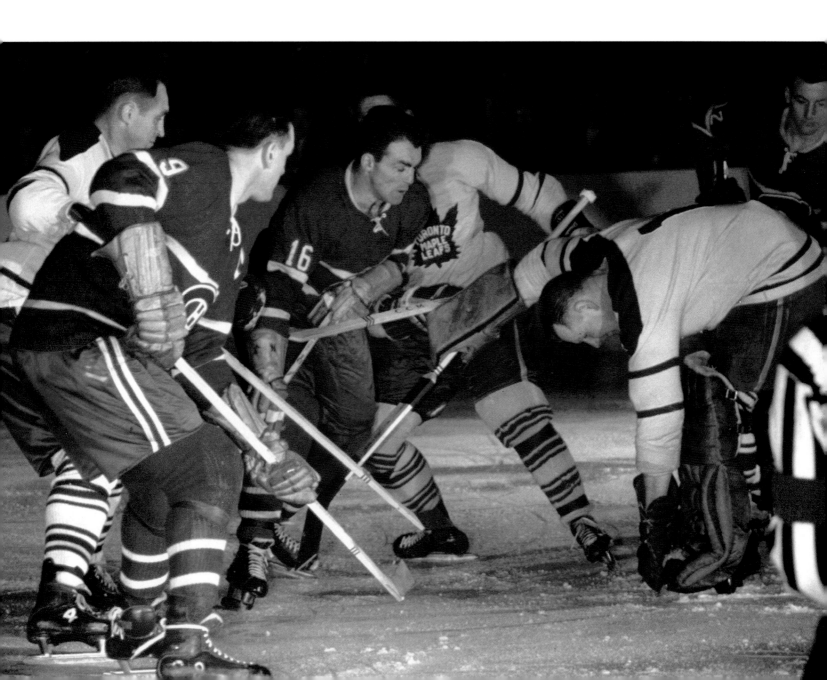

J. C. TREMBLAY

After Montreal's era of five straight Stanley Cup victories, their core of defensemen was slowly dismantled. With each passing year holdovers such as Bob Turner, Dollard St. Laurent, Doug Harvey, Al Langlois and Tom Johnson left the team. The new wave of Canadiens' defensemen started with the addition of Jean-Claude Tremblay. He was soon followed by Jacques Laperriere, Ted Harris and Terry Harper. This group would serve as the nucleus of defenders that would win five Stanley Cups between 1965 and 1971.

J.C. Tremblay's first full season with the Canadiens was in 1961-62. Before he was promoted to the NHL, Tremblay played in the Montreal farm system with the Hull-Ottawa Canadiens of the Eastern Professional Hockey League. He was named the EPHL's most valuable player in 1959-60. He split the 1960-61 season between Hull-Ottawa and the big club in Montreal. Never a physical defenseman (his highest penalty minute total in one season was 24), Tremblay relied on his skating and puck control to play a finesse game.

This style of play proved to be effective for Tremblay. In the 1965 Finals, Tremblay had 10

points as the Canadiens won the Stanley Cup. In 1966, Tremblay's playoff point total of 11 placed him behind only Norm Ullman of Detroit. He received strong consideration for the Conn Smythe Trophy which went to Detroit's Roger Crozier. A first team all-star in 1970-71 when he had a career high of 63 points, Tremblay added 17 points in the 1971 playoffs as he won his final Stanley Cup with the Canadiens.

By 1972-73, Tremblay moved on to the Quebec Nordiques where he played for seven seasons. Tremblay's sweater number (3) is only one of two retired by the Nordiques in their history.

	Born: 1-22-1939, Bagotville, Quebec				
	Height: 5'11" Weight: 190 Shot: Left Position: Defense				
	Sweater # 3 Years Played: 1959 - 1972				
	Teams: Montreal, Quebec				
	GP	G	A	PTS	PM
	794	57	306	363	204
Playoffs:	108	14	51	65	58

Above: J.C. Tremblay (3) moves away from Toronto's Ron Ellis (6).

Opposite: Tremblay helps the Montreal netminder defend against Leafs' Dick Duff.

JOHN FERGUSON

Above: John Ferguson (22) was on five Stanley Cup winning teams in his career.

By 1963 the management of the Montreal Canadiens knew they had to get a player with a physical presence on the ice. Their talented but smallish forwards were getting pushed around far too often. Their search for that player took them to Cleveland of the AHL where they found 25 year old John Ferguson. The intimidation of the Canadiens was about to end.

In his rookie year of 1963-64, John Ferguson played in 59 games, scoring 18 times and assisting on 27 others. Just as noteworthy was his 125 minutes in penalties as he fought players like Ted Green, Ed Westfall, Ron Stewart and Bob Nevin. He finished second in rookie of the year honours to teammate Jacques Laperriere but his mark was made on the NHL.

During his career with Montreal between 1963 and 1971, the Canadiens won five Stanley Cups. In 1968-69 Ferguson recorded a career high 29 goals and 52 points and he scored the Stanley Cup winning goal against St. Louis in the 1969 Finals.

Born: 9-5-1938, Vancouver, British Columbia				
Height: 5'11" Weight: 190 Shot: left Position: Left Wing				
Sweater # 22 Years Played:1963 - 1971				
Teams: Montreal				
GP	G	A	PTS	PM
500	145	158	303	944
Playoffs: 85	20	18	38	260

DOUG HARVEY

Above: Doug Harvey battles Toronto's Bert Olmstead behind the Montreal net.

Doug Harvey was the first defenseman in NHL history who "quarterbacked" his team. Playing from the blueline, Harvey could orchestrate the Canadiens style of "fire wagon hockey" with his ability to frame accurate passes. Not only was his passing a sight to behold but he could control the game as he pleased.

A great all round athlete who might have had a career in baseball, Harvey joined the Canadiens after playing senior hockey with the Montreal Royals. The awards started coming Harvey's way shortly afterwards. He won the Norris Trophy a total of seven times between 1955 and 1962. His only miss was in 1959 when teammate Tom Johnson won the award. During those same years, Harvey was named to the first all-star team ten times. He helped the

Canadiens to six Stanley Cups before he moved to the New York Rangers.

The great defenseman left the Canadiens to become a player-coach with the Rangers for the 1961-62 season. He continued his fine play leading the Broadway club to a playoff appearance and won his final Norris Trophy.

Born: 12-19-1924, Montreal, Quebec				
Height: 5'11" Weight: 180 Shot: Left Position: Defense				
Sweater # 2 Years Played: 1947 - 1969				
Teams: Montreal, New York Rangers, Detroit,St. Louis				
GP	G	A	PTS	PM
1113	88	452	540	1168
Playoffs: 137	8	64	72	152

CHARLIE HODGE

Above: Charlie Hodge (1) stops a shot from Toronto's Frank Mahovlich.

Goaltender Charlie Hodge was never quite sure he would make it to the NHL. At one point, as he struggled in the minors, Hodge nearly left the game for good. He had reached this point after a rather poor 1956-57 season with Rochester of the American Hockey League when he posted a 3.22 goals against average in 41 games. With Jacques Plante in Montreal, Hodge was essentially the number two goalie in the Canadiens system.

The Canadiens traded Plante in June, 1963 and received goalie Gump Worsley in return from the New York Rangers. Although Worsley started the 1963-64 season in Montreal, Hodge had made a great impression at training camp. When Worsley faltered, Hodge got the call and responded by posting a league high eight shutouts and was named

winner of the Vezina Trophy. Hodge was in the NHL to stay.

Hodge played in 52 games in 1964-65 as the Canadiens won their first Stanley Cup in five years. In 1965-66, Hodge shared a Vezina Trophy with Gump Worsley. He finished his NHL career with the Oakland Seals and the Vancouver Canucks.

Born: 7-28-1933, Lachine, Quebec
Height: 5'6"   Weight: 150   Shot: Left   Position: Goalie
Sweater # 1   Years Played: 1954 - 1971
Teams: Montreal, Oakland, Vancouver

	GP	W	L	T	AVG	SO
	358	152	124	60	2.71	24
Playoffs: 16	6	8	-		2.31	2

DICKIE MOORE

Above: Dickie Moore (12) gets help from teammate Jean Guy Talbot against Toronto's Bob Nevin.

If there was a player who could play with pain, it had to be Dickie Moore of the Montreal Canadiens. Injuries plagued his career, and it nearly cost him his job with the Canadiens as they seriously thought of trading him. Bad knees, shoulder problems, and broken wrists and hands all added to Moore's woes. But Moore was one of hockey's toughest competitors and as he regained his health, his production rose to significant levels.

He became the NHL scoring leader for two years in row in 1958 and 1959. In the 1958-59 season, Moore set a NHL record with 96 points with 41 goals and 55 assists (edging Gordie Howe's previous mark of 95). This feat was truly amazing considering Moore played with a cast on an injured wrist. Such an effort was typical of Moore who would sacrifice his body for a win. Not afraid of anyone, Moore battled frequently with the likes of Detroit's

tough guy "Terrible" Ted Lindsay. Moore also became the first player in NHL history to record six points in one playoff game when he had two goals and four assists in an 8-1 Montreal win over Boston on March 25, 1954. In total, he played on six Stanley Cup winning teams with the Canadiens and made the first all-star team twice in his career.

Born: 1-6-1931, Montreal, Quebec					
Height: 5'10" Weight: 185 Shot: Right Position: Right Wing					
Sweater # 12 Years Played: 1951 - 1968					
Teams: Montreal, Toronto, St. Louis					
	GP	G	A	PTS	PM
	719	261	347	608	652
Playoffs:	135	46	64	110	122

BOBBY ROUSSEAU

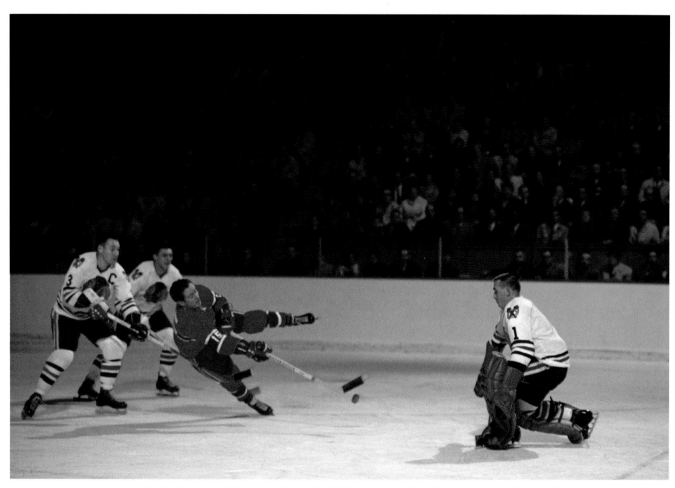

Above: Bobby Rousseau (15) takes a shot while falling down against Chicago's Denis DeJordy (1).

If Bobby Rousseau had one ambition in life it was to play hockey for the Montreal Canadiens. As a 12 year-old he was presented with a trophy by Canadiens great Bernie Geoffrion. Rousseau hoped that one day they would be teammates, and nine years later, he realized his dream.

Rousseau made it to the Canadiens for 15 games in 1960-61, and played his first full season in 1961-62 responding with 21 goals and 24 assists, taking the Calder Trophy as top rookie. On February 1, 1964 Rousseau had the greatest game of his career with five goals against the Detroit Red Wings.

During the 1964-65 playoffs, Rousseau started to play like a star. He scored five goals and had a total of 12 points to finish third in playoff scoring behind Beliveau and Bobby Hull of Chicago.

Rousseau's game was built around his skating speed and strong defensive abilities. Having a good slapshot allowed Rousseau to be quite effective on the power play and his checking talents made him a top penalty killer. His NHL career ended with the New York Rangers who made a trip to the Stanley Cup Finals in 1972.

	Born: 7-26-1940, Montreal, Quebec				
Height: 5'10" Weight: 178 Shot: Right Position: Right Wing					
Sweater # 15 Years Played: 1960 - 1975					
Teams: Montreal, Minnesota, New York Rangers					
	GP	G	A	PTS	PM
	942	245	458	703	359
Playoffs:	128	27	57	84	69

JEAN GUY TALBOT

Above: Jean Guy Talbot leads a rush up the ice.

As a youngster, Jean Guy Talbot idolized the great Doug Harvey and tried to play like him. Talbot became a rushing defenseman as a junior, but when he made it to the Canadiens he had to become more defensive. His mobility and quickness made him a difficult defender to beat in one-on-one situations. Harvey showed Talbot how to play in the NHL giving the youngster the confidence he needed to succeed.

Talbot's best season was in 1961-62 when he was named to the NHL's first all-star team. He notched a career high 42 assists and 47 points which was quite high for a Canadiens defenseman. Ironically enough, Talbot's partner on the first all-star team was Doug Harvey who by then had moved to the New York Rangers.

As Talbot broke into the Canadiens lineup, the club went on a streak of five consecutive Stanley Cups. He stayed around to help new defensemen like Jacques Laperriere and J.C. Tremblay get their feet wet in the NHL. Talbot was a part of two more Cup wins in 1965 and 1966.

Born: 7-11-1932, Cap Madelaine, Quebec
Height: 5'11" Weight: 170 Shot: Left Position: Defense
Sweater # 17   Years Played: 1954 - 1971
Teams: Montreal, Minnesota, Detroit, St. Louis, Buffalo

	GP	G	A	PTS	PM
	1056	43	242	285	1006
Playoffs:	150	4	26	30	142

NEW YORK RANGERS

At the best of times New York is never an easy place to play in. Lose and the fans let you know it. The tough, demanding patrons of Madison Square Garden could certainly make life miserable for a losing hockey team. The Rangers already played second fiddle to the baseball Giants and Yankees, the football Giants, and the basketball Knicks. Even though the Rangers were not a good team prior to 1967, the Garden was usually filled for NHL hockey, and often the fans did not like what they saw and voiced their displeasure.

The last time the Stanley Cup was seen in New York was back in 1940 when the Rangers beat the Maple Leafs in a six-game Final. In the years between 1940 and 1955, the Rangers missed the playoffs 11 times. Only once did they return to the Finals, in 1950 when they lost to Detroit in seven games. The Broadway Blueshirts made it back to the playoffs for three years in a row starting in 1955-56 but could never get past the Semi-Final round. In 1958-59, the Rangers held the fourth playoff spot by seven points with only five games remaining. In a remarkable collapse, the Rangers won only one game the rest of the way, and the Maple Leafs surged to take the final playoff spot. In 1959-60, New York finished in sixth and last place.

The Rangers' descent to the bottom of the league was surprising. They had a core of good players that their farm system had produced in the early Fifties. Some of their better players were Andy Bathgate, Harry Howell, Gump Worsley, Camille Henry, Ron Murphy, Dean Prentice and Lou Fontinato. In addition they picked up quality defensemen in Bill Gadsby and Allan Stanley, and a consistent forward in Andy Hebenton. Many of these players made it to the Hockey Hall of Fame, but except for Howell and Bathgate, had their best moments with other teams. The Rangers could not develop or acquire enough role players to help out their stars. In addition, the Rangers were generally a small team that did not play aggressively. Soon the Rangers and the Boston Bruins settled into a battle for last place every year from 1959 to 1967.

New York general manager Muzz Patrick tried to reverse the losing trends but with little success. He went through a series of

Right: Lorne "Gump" Worsley kicks a shot away from Toronto's Bob Pulford (20).

coaches (Phil Watson, Alf Pike, Red Sullivan) and even tried going behind the bench himself, all to no avail. Patrick then went out and acquired Montreal's great defenseman, Doug Harvey, to be a playing coach for the 1961-62 season. It worked for one year with Harvey winning the Norris Trophy and the Rangers making the playoffs. New York extended the eventual champion, Toronto to six games in the Semi-Finals. The Rangers brought in more former Canadiens when they acquired Phil Goyette, Don Marshall, and finally the great Jacques Plante. But the Rangers still missed the playoffs.

In 1964, Emile "the Cat" Francis was installed as general manager. As soon as he took over the top job, he addressed the issues of size and skill. He gave Vic Hadfield, a big winger with a mean streak, a chance to play regularly. He added Jim Neilson on defense, and gave more action to forwards like Rod Gilbert and Jean Ratelle. Also, Bernie Geoffrion was brought back to play for the Rangers after a two year retirement from the Montreal Canadiens. More muscle was added in the form of

Above: A blizzard of Ranger sweaters surround Toronto's Johnny Bower.

Opposite: Rod Gilbert forechecks aggressively deep in the Toronto Maple Leaf's end.

Reggie Fleming and Orland Kurtenbach.

A major trade with Toronto saw New York add Bob Nevin, Arnie Brown and Rod Seiling. They also gave up four players to Providence of the AHL for goaltender Eddie Giacomin. In 1966-67, Giacomin made the first all-star team and led the league in shutouts. With their goaltending and defense solidified, the Rangers relied on goals from Gilbert, Hadfield and Ratelle. Nevin became a leader on the team (eventually he was named captain) and he worked well with Don Marshall and Phil Goyette. Slowly, the Rangers started to find the winning habit.

The 1966-67 season saw the Rangers make it to the playoffs although they were knocked out in four straight by the Montreal Canadiens. By 1967-68, the Rangers were a force to be reckoned with as they finished second with 90 points. In 1972, the Rangers made it all the way back to the Finals before losing to Bobby Orr and the Boston Bruins. The days of being the league doormat were over. However, the Rangers have not sipped from the Stanley Cup since 1940!

ANDY BATHGATE

Opposite: Toronto's Tim Horton keeps an eye on Ranger captain Andy Bathgate.

Left: Bathgate was named as the league's most valuable player in 1959.

It's not often that the NHL's most valuable player is on a team that misses the playoffs. In 1958-59, the New York Rangers suffered a late season collapse and were edged out of the playoffs by Toronto on the final night of the season. However, it was Ranger center Andy Bathgate that took away the Hart Trophy. His 40-goal, 48-assist performance could not go unnoticed.

Bathgate's play always had a high impact on the New York team. One of the greatest players in the history of the Rangers, Bathgate ran off a streak of seven consecutive years where he recorded more than 70 scoring points. By the time Bathgate left the Rangers, he held many New York single season and career records. For example, Bathgate held the Rangers' career mark for most goals (272), assists (457) and points (729). He also set an NHL record by scoring a goal in ten consecutive games. Bathgate was a clever playmaker who always seemed to find the right spot on the ice to work his magic. His hard shot was also compared to that of Bobby Hull and Bernie Geoffrion.

A clear leader on the team, the Rangers named Bathgate captain in 1961 which he retained until traded to Toronto in February, 1964. The Rangers sought an influx of young players when they sent Bathgate and Don McKenney to the Leafs for Bob Nevin, Dick Duff, Arnie Brown, Bill Collins and Rod Seiling. Toronto paid a high price but the Maple Leafs felt Bathgate would help them win a third consecutive Stanley Cup.

Toronto was not disappointed with Bathgate who recorded nine points in 14 playoff games. He scored the Stanley Cup winning goal against Detroit's Terry Sawchuk in a 4 - 0 win in game seven of the 1964 Finals.

In May, 1965 Toronto sent Bathgate to Detroit as part of an eight-player deal. The Pittsburgh Penguins selected Bathgate in the 1967 expansion draft. He played his last NHL season in 1970-71.

Born: 8-28-1932, Winnipeg, Manitoba

Height: 6'   Weight: 180   Shot: Right   Position: Right Wing

Sweater # 9   Years Played: 1952 - 1971

Teams: New York Rangers, Toronto, Detroit, Pittsburgh

	GP	G	A	PTS	PM
	1069	349	624	973	624
Playoffs:	54	21	14	35	56

ROD GILBERT

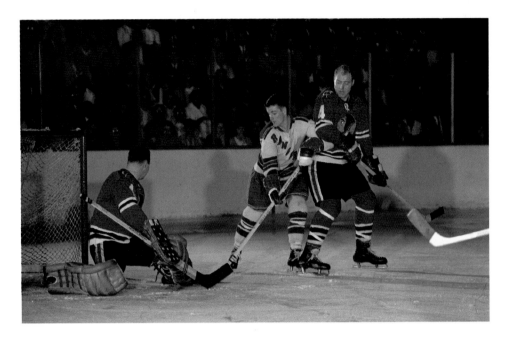

Rod Gilbert's promising career was nearly cut short because of a severe back problem. His injury could be traced to a junior game in 1961 when he tripped over some debris on the ice and crashed into the boards. He eventually needed spinal fusion to correct the problem causing him to miss almost all of the 1961-62 season. He returned to play hockey wearing a corset to protect his back, but in 1965 needed a second major operation. The Montreal native fought bravely to overcome his injury and went on to complete a great career with the New York Rangers.

Named as the OHA's most valuable player in 1960-61 (54 goals and 103 points) when he played in the Rangers' system at Guelph, Gilbert's arrival was very much anticipated in the Big Apple. Gilbert got his first prolonged action during the 1962 playoffs against Toronto. In four games, Gilbert scored two goals and three assists as the Rangers extended the Maple Leafs to six games. Gilbert's playoff performance clearly showed he had star potential. By his third full season, Gilbert led the Rangers in goals scored (25) and points (61). He also predicted he would play his entire career in New York and would score over 400 career goals.

By the time he was done, Gilbert had accomplished what he had set out to do. He played in 18 seasons for the Rangers and holds the club career record for most goals (406), assists (615) and points (1021). He had his best year in 1971-72 when he scored 43 goals and 97 points and was a selection on the first all-star team as the league's best right winger. The Rangers made it to the Finals in 1972 and he contributed 15 points in 16 games, although Boston edged the Rangers for the Cup.

Gilbert's perseverance was recognized in 1976 when he won the Masterton Trophy. He received the ultimate reward for a great career when he was elected to the Hall of Fame in 1982.

	GP	G	A	PTS	PM
	1065	406	615	1021	508
Playoffs:	79	34	33	67	43

Born: 7-1-1941, Montreal, Quebec
Height: 5'9" Weight: 180 Shot: Right Position: Right Wing
Sweater # 7   Years Played: 1960 - 1978
Teams: New York Rangers

Above: Rod Gilbert gets behind Chicago's Elmer Vasko to get a shot at goalie Glenn Hall.

Opposite: Gilbert holds a variety of Ranger all-time team records.

VIC HADFIELD

The New York Rangers had a rather small team in the early Sixties. Their better players could find the going a little rough on the ice. The Rangers knew they had to remedy the situation and they started to scout for players who were big and aggressive. They found such a player in left winger Vic Hadfield in the Chicago system, and in 1961, they drafted him away from the Blackhawks and gained a hardnosed cornerman.

In his early days, Hadfield was short on finesse but long on abrasiveness. When he first broke into the NHL in 1961-62, he battled players like Bob Baun, Ted Green, Tim Horton and Henri Richard. He played his first full season in 1963-64 when he scored 14 goals and 25 points, but unfortunately he also had 151 penalty minutes which was the most in the NHL. Hadfield was playing the game the way his idol Ted Lindsay used to, and it was gaining him respect throughout the league. His name would come up constantly in trade talks, but the Rangers would always turn down any offers for the 6-foot, 180-pound Hadfield.

As his ice time increased, Hadfield began to score goals and learned to pick his spots to display toughness. In 1967-68, Hadfield scored 20 goals for the first time in his career. He would score over 20

for the next eight seasons. Hadfield's best year was in 1971-72 when he scored 50 goals (the first and only Ranger ever to do so). Playing with Rod Gilbert and Jean Ratelle on the GAG (Goal-a-Game) line, he added 56 assists and was named to the second all-star team.

Hadfield's leadership skills were recognized in 1971 when he was named captain. He was selected for Team Canada in 1972, playing in two games against the Russians. Hadfield was with the Rangers until 1974 when he was dealt to the Penguins. He completed two 30 goal seasons in Pittsburgh before he retired in 1977.

		Born: 10-4-1940, Oakville, Ontario			
Height: 6' Weight: 190 Shot: Left Position: Left Wing					
Sweater # 11 Years Played: 1961 - 1977					
Teams: New York Rangers, Pittsburgh					
	GP	G	A	PTS	PM
	1002	323	389	712	1154
Playoffs:	74	27	21	48	117

Above: Vic Hadfield faces another hard nosed player in Toronto's Bobby Baun.

Opposite: Hadfield was the first Ranger to score 50 goals in a season.

HARRY HOWELL

It took until the 1966-67 season for New York Ranger defenseman Harry Howell to finally get some of the recognition he deserved. He was awarded the James Norris Trophy and was named to the NHL's first all-star team for his 12 goal and 40 point total. He may have been the last defensive defenseman to win the Norris, because the award took a different tone when Bobby Orr won it for the first time in 1968.

Howell made his debut with New York in 1952-53 after his junior career with the Guelph Biltmores

of the OHA. He played in only one minor league game before going off to New York.

Although he was not abrasive, Howell was nonetheless effective in his own end. A smooth, deft skater, Howell showed offensive talent by recording over 20 assists for six consecutive seasons between 1962 and 1968. His highest assist total was 31 in 1963-64. His style of play made him a durable performer missing only 20 games in his first 16 years with the Rangers! At the end of his career in New York, Howell held the Ranger career mark for

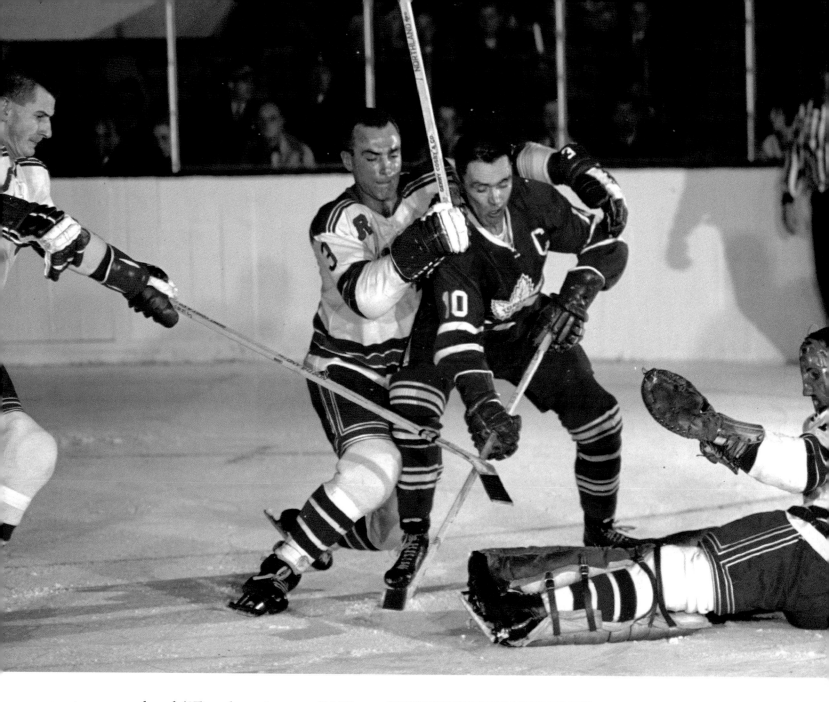

most seasons played (17) and most games (1160). Despite his size of 6-foot and 200 pounds he was penalized 100 minutes only once in his 21 year career.

The leadership qualities of Howell were acknowledged by the Rangers who named him captain in 1955, a title he kept for two years. In May, 1965 the Rangers named Howell as playing assistant coach. In 1969, the Rangers sold Howell to the Oakland Seals who in turn sold him to the Los Angeles Kings in 1971. He played with the Kings until the end of the 1972-73 season.

In 1979, Howell was elected to the Hall of Fame.

	Born: 12-28-1932, Hamilton, Ontario				
	Height: 6'1" Weight: 200 Shot: Left Position: Defense				
	Sweater # 3 Years Played: 1952 - 1973				
	Teams: New York Rangers, Oakland, Los Angeles				
	GP	**G**	**A**	**PTS**	**PM**
	1411	94	324	418	1298
Playoffs:	38	3	3	6	32

Opposite: Harry Howell won the Norris Trophy as the league's top defenseman in 1967.

Above: Howell has a hold on Toronto's George Armstrong (10) in front of the Ranger net.

JEAN RATELLE

Quebec-born Jean Ratelle idolized Montreal Canadiens' star Jean Beliveau and always a dreamed of someday playing with his hero. But this wasn't to happen because Ratelle and friend Rod Gilbert signed at the same time with the Guelph Biltmores, a team sponsored by the New York Rangers. Both Ratelle and Gilbert were labelled as "can't-miss" prospects, especially after the 1960-61 season when they finished first and second in the OHA scoring race (103 points for Gilbert and 101 for Ratelle, including a league high 61 assists).

Ironically, both players would suffer severe back injuries which would threaten their careers.

While Gilbert jumped to the Rangers quickly, it took Ratelle a little longer to become a regular. He split four seasons between the Rangers and the minor leagues before he finally stuck for good in 1964-65. He nearly didn't get his chance when a contract dispute almost had Ratelle going to the Milwaukee Braves to pursue a baseball career. He also thought of becoming a professional golfer before Ranger general manager Emile Francis cor-

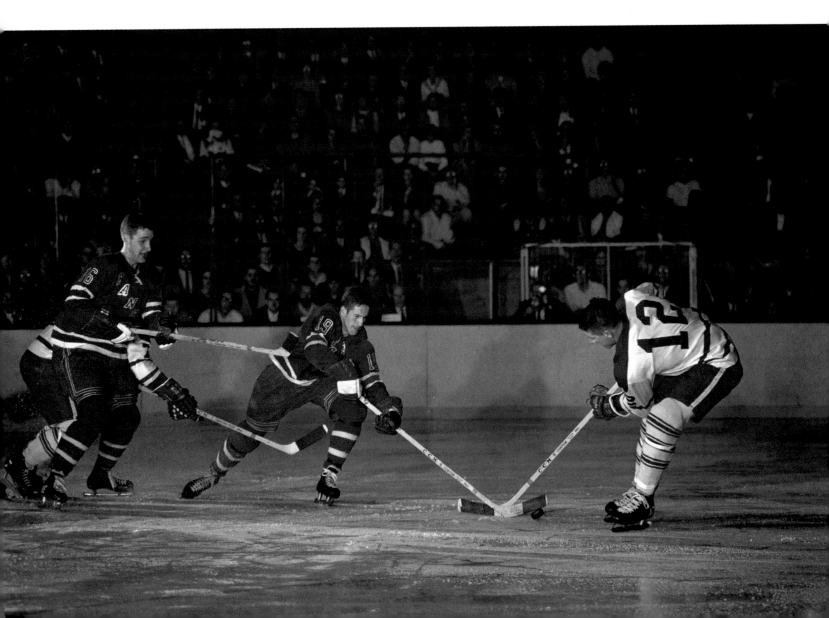

rected the money situation to Ratelle's satisfaction. An injury to center Phil Goyette gave Ratelle steady work and an opportunity to be reunited with Gilbert. It was the turning point in Ratelle's career.

In his first full season, 1965-66, Ratelle scored 21 times showing his good goal scoring abilities. By 1967-68, Ratelle had 32 goals and 78 points as the Rangers started to become a power in the NHL. With Vic Hadfield added to his line, Ratelle produced a 109 point season in 1971-72. It was the first time a Ranger had passed the 100 point mark.

Always a clean and gentlemanly player, Ratelle won the Lady Byng Trophy twice and the Masterton Trophy once. After a blockbuster trade to Boston in 1975, Ratelle had six seasons of more than 25 goals and passed the 100 point total once more in 1975-76. He played a large role in the Bruins making it to the Finals in 1977 and 1978.

Above: Jean Ratelle and Marcel Pronovost race for a loose puck.

Opposite: Ratelle (19) steals the puck from Toronto's Peter Stemkowski (12).

Born: 10-3-1940, Lac St. Jean, Quebec					
Height: 6'1" Weight: 180 Shot: Left Position: Center					
Sweater # 19 Years Played: 1960 - 1981					
Teams: New York Rangers, Boston					
	GP	G	A	PTS	PM
	1281	491	776	1267	276
Playoffs:	123	32	66	98	24

GUMP WORSLEY

Lorne "Gump" Worsley began his career with New York Ranger teams whose defense provided little protection for the goalie. While still in New York, Worsley was once asked which team gave him the most trouble. "The Rangers!", Worsley replied. Gump was of course thrilled when he was dealt to the Canadiens in June, 1963.

Worsley's career actually got off to a good start in 1952-53 when he played in 50 games for the Rangers and posted a 3.06 goals-against average. Even though this performance won him the Calder Trophy as best rookie, Worsley found himself back in the minors for the 1953-54 season. It marked his sixth year in the minor leagues. He was named the most valuable player in the WHL when he played for the Vancouver Canucks and it earned him a ticket back to New York. He was with the Rangers until 1963 when he was sent to Montreal for Jacques Plante – a trade which he thought would give his career a new start.

However, in 1963-64 Worsley played in only seven regular season games (spending most of the year with the Quebec Aces of the AHL) losing the starter's job to Charlie Hodge. In 1964-65, Worsley played in only 18 games during the season but came on during the playoffs to record two shut-outs, including a 4 - 0 win in game seven of the Finals against Chicago. Worsley had the first of four Stanley Cup rings and his minor league days were finally over!

In his career with the Canadiens, Worsley shared two Vezina Trophies with Charlie Hodge in 1966 and 1968. He had the league's best goals-against average at 1.98 in 1967-68, when he also recorded six shutouts. Worsley did not look ath-letic, but he had great reflexes and the agility to make his flopping style effective.

Sold to Minnesota in 1970, Worsley played over four seasons with the North Stars. He decided to wear a mask in only his last NHL season, 1973-74. His long professional career was recognized with his election to the Hall of Fame in 1980.

Below: Gump Worsley is in good position to stop a shot from Toronto's Bob Nevin (11).

Opposite: Worsley never had an easy time playing for the Rangers.

Born: 5-14-1929, Montreal, Quebec
Height: 5'7" Weight: 180 Shot: Left Position: Goalie
Sweater # 1 Years Played: 1952 - 1974
Teams: New York Rangers, Montreal, Minnesota

GP	W	L	T	AVG	SO
862	335	353	150	2.90	43
70	41	25	-	2.82	5

ED GIACOMIN

Above: Ed Giacomin has company in his crease with Chicago's Doug Mohns (2).

Goaltender Ed Giacomin got his start in professional hockey by impersonating his older brother at a tryout for Washington of EHL. The fraud was forgotten by the coach when he realized how good the younger Giacomin was, and signed him up.

After seven years in the minors, the New York Rangers bought him from the Providence Reds for four players and $75,000. It seemed like a high price at the time, but Giacomin proved it was a good investment by staying with the Rangers for the next 10 years. In his first full year as a starter with the Rangers, he recorded a league-high nine shutouts and a 2.61 goals-against average. He was named to the first all-star team.

Quick with his hands and legs, Giacomin's acrobatic style made him very popular with the huge New York crowds. He also liked to roam from his net to play the puck, and on occasion take a shot at

an empty net. In 1970-71 Giacomin had a sparkling 2.15 goals-against average and shared the Vezina Trophy with Gilles Villemure.

Giacomin's sweater number (1) has been retired by the Rangers and he was elected to the Hall of Fame in 1987.

Born: 6-6-1939, Sudbury, Ontario
Height: 5'11" Weight: 180 Shot: Right Position: Goalie
Sweater Number: 1   Years Played: 1965 to 1978
Teams: New York Rangers, Detroit

	GP	W	L	T	Avg.	SO
	160	289	206	97	2.82	54
Playoffs:	65	29	35		2.82	1

PHIL GOYETTE

Above: Phil Goyette was acquired from the Montreal Canadiens in June 1963.

Phil Goyette's biggest problem when he was with the Montreal Canadiens was having to play behind Jean Beliveau, Henri Richard and Ralph Backstrom. When he made the Canadiens in 1956-57, the club was so well-heeled there was little for Goyette to do but to become a defensive specialist. It was only when he left Montreal that his offensive skills surfaced.

He played very little for Montreal that year but made a contibution by scoring two goals in the playoffs. It was the first of four consecutive titles for Goyette.

In June, 1963 Goyette was part of a big trade between the Canadiens and the New York Rangers. After scoring only 12 goals in his last two years in Montreal, Goyette scored 24 times in his first year with the Rangers. Playing with Don Marshall and Bob Nevin, Goyette recorded over 60 points three times. He scored a career high 25 goals in 1967-68 and matched his best point total of 65.

A smooth playmaker and top face-off man throughout his career, Goyette was named as the first coach of the New York Islanders.

Born: 10-31-1933, Lachine, Quebec					
Height: 5'11" Weight: 170 Shot: Left Position: Center					
Sweater # 20 Years Played: 1956 - 1972					
Teams: Montreal, New York Rangers, St. Louis, Buffalo					
	GP	**G**	**A**	**PTS**	**PM**
	940	207	467	674	131
Playoffs:	94	17	29	46	26

CAMILLE HENRY

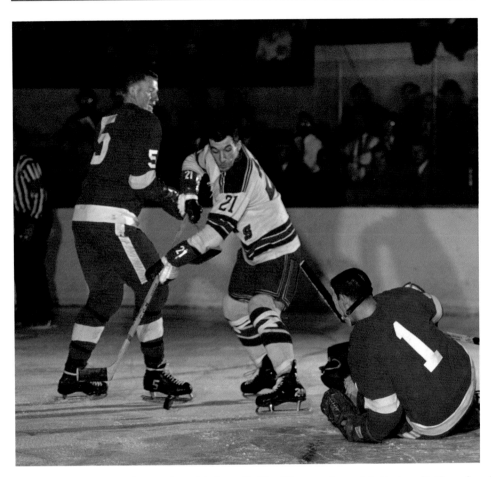

Above: Camille Henry (21) wrestles past Detroit's Doug Barkley (5) to get the puck behind goalie Terry Sawchuk (1).

Camille Henry made quite a debut with the New York Rangers in 1953-54. As a rookie in the NHL, the small center scored 24 goals and 39 points in 66 games. He also had a four-goal game against Detroit's Terry Sawchuk. Henry was awarded the Calder Trophy but after just 21 games the following year, he was back in the minor leagues. He played another two years in the AHL with Providence before he earned his way back to the NHL.

Only 5'8" and 150 pounds, Henry was a swift skater who, despite his small stature, could play well in traffic. His sense of anticipation, hard shot and touch around the net helped him to score 227 goals in his first eight NHL seasons. Henry was especially good on the power play where he had a knack for deflecting shots into the net. In his first full season back with the Rangers, Henry scored 32 goals and won his second major award, the Lady

Byng Trophy. He was named to the second all-star team and was back to stay.

Henry's best season with New York was in 1962-63 when he scored 37 goals and had 60 points. His goal total was only one behind league leader Gordie Howe. In 1963-64, he played on the all-French line for the Rangers with Rod Gilbert and Phil Goyette, scoring 29 goals and 56 points.

Born: 1-31-1933, Quebec City, Quebec
Height: 5'8" Weight: 152 Shot: Left Position: Center
Sweater # 21   Years Played: 1953 - 1970
Teams: New York Rangers, Chicago, St. Louis

	GP	G	A	PTS	PM
	727	279	249	528	88
Playoffs:	47	6	12	18	7

DON MARSHALL

Above: Marshall tries to pin Toronto's Dave Keon against the boards.

Born in Verdun, Quebec, Don Marshall played his junior hockey in Montreal where he was captain of the junior Canadiens of the QJHL.In 1954-55, he saw his first action with the senior Canadiens. He played in 39 games and scored five goals.

The 1955-56 season was his first full season in the NHL, and it also marked the first of five consecutive Stanley Cup years for him. Marshall's best goal-scoring year in Montreal was in 1957-58 when he had 22. He was a hard worker for the power-house Canadiens team and didn't complain about his utility role. A good skater and clean player (only 127 career penalty minutes), Marshall was a consistent performer when called upon.

His work habits certainly impressed the New York Rangers who had this top penalty killer included in a trade that sent Gump Worsley to Mon-treal for Marshall, Jacques Plante and Phil Goyette. Like Goyette, Marshall found a more offensive role in New York producing four seasons of 20 or more goals. His best year for the Rangers was in 1965-66 when he scored 24 goals and 54 points. In 1966-67, he scored 24 times and was named to the NHL's second all-star team.

	Born: 3-23-1932, Verdun, Quebec				
	Height: 5'10" Weight: 166 Shot: Left Position: Left Wing				
	Sweater # 22 Years Played: 1951 - 1972				
	Teams: Montreal, New York Rangers, Buffalo, Toronto				
	GP	G	A	PTS	PM
	1176	265	324	589	127
Playoffs:	94	8	15	23	14

JIM NEILSON

Above: Jim Neilson (15) tries to beat Blackhawks' Chico Maki to the puck.

Born in Big River, Saskatchewan Jim Neilson never lived on a reservation even though he was proud to be of Indian ancestry. At 6'2" and 205 pounds, Neilson was ideally suited to play hockey as a defenseman.

In spite of his size, Neilson was not especially physical for a defenseman. A good skater, Neilson liked to carry the puck out of his own end and use his excellent passing skills. His crisp, hard shot earned him a few goals in the NHL (he scored a career high of 10 in 1968-69). In his first season 1962-63, he was paired with the great Doug Harvey, and it took a while before he found his own niche.

As the Rangers improved in the late Sixties, Neilson started to take charge. In 1967-68, his six goals and 29 assists combined with his all-round play, earned Neilson a berth on the NHL's second all-star team. In 1971-72, Neilson had another good year with seven goals and 37 points in leading the Rangers to the Stanley Cup Finals.

Born: 11-28-1941, Big River, Saskatchewan
Height: 6'2" Weight: 205 Shot: Left Position: Defense
Sweater # 15 Years Played: 1962 - 1978
Teams: New York Rangers, California, Cleveland

	GP	G	A	PTS	PM
	1023	69	299	368	904
Playoffs:	65	2	16	18	61

BOB NEVIN

Above: Bob Nevin is watched by Boston's Don Awrey (26).

Bob Nevin began his hockey career in the Toronto Maple Leaf minor system and stepped up the the NHL in 1960. In his rookie year he scored 21 goals and 58 points playing on a line with Red Kelly and Frank Mahovlich. In Nevin's second and third year with the Leafs, they captured two consecutive Stanley Cups. He played a major checking role in both victories.

Nevin developed into a tireless skater and one of the top defensive wingers in the league. His nose for the net made him a valuable and consistent two-way forward. In 1964 the Leafs traded him to the New York Rangers. He missed out on a third straight Stanley Cup win, but the change of scenery was good for Nevin in the long run.

With the Rangers, Nevin was named captain of the team in 1965, and he scored over 20 goals in five of his seven years. His best goal-scoring year was in 1968-69 when he netted 31 for the Rangers. Dealt to the Minnesota North Stars in May, 1971, Nevin moved on to the Los Angeles Kings in 1973. Playing in all 80 games in 1974-75, Nevin had a career-best 31 goals and 72 points.

	Born: 3-18-1938, South Porcupine, Ontario				
	Height: 6' Weight: 190 Shot: Right Position: Right Wing				
	Sweater # 8 Years Played: 1957 - 1976				
	Teams: Toronto, New York Rangers, Minnesota, Los Angeles				
	GP	**G**	**A**	**PTS**	**PM**
	1128	307	419	726	211
Playoffs:	84	16	18	34	24

TORONTO MAPLE LEAFS

When Bill Barilko scored in overtime on April 21, 1951 against Montreal, it gave the Toronto Maple Leafs their fourth Stanley Cup in five years, and it looked as though the Toronto dynasty might last a few more seasons. However, in August, 1951 a plane Barilko was riding in went missing while he was on a fishing trip. The untimely death of Barilko cost the Leafs the heart of their defense and propelled the Toronto club down a very dark road between 1952 and 1958. During those years, the Leafs never finished higher than third and missed the playoffs three times. The once proud franchise had fallen upon hard times.

Toronto was still floundering in November, 1958 when a new executive decided to take action. George "Punch" Imlach had joined the Leafs the previous June as assistant general manager. Sensing that the team needed some dramatic changes, Imlach asked to be made general manager. Once installed, he fired coach Billy Reay and put himself behind the bench. It was the start of a great decade for the Maple Leafs with Imlach in complete control.

Imlach's first task was to get Toronto into the playoffs even though the Leafs were in last place with a 5-12-3 record to start the 1958-59 season. A positive thinker, Imlach felt there was a chance to make the post season if they could play better hockey. The Leafs did improve, and by the final game of the season trailed the New York Rangers by only one game. On that final night, the Montreal Canadiens knocked off the Rangers 4 - 2 while the Leafs rallied to beat Detroit 6 - 4. The victory gave Imlach a 22-20-8 record as coach and more importantly, a playoff spot with 65 points to New York's 64. What a miracle finish! Toronto's Cinderella story only ended in the Finals when Montreal took the Stanley Cup in five games.

The change in Leaf fortunes came about as a result of an influx of youth and the acquisition of key veterans by Imlach through trades. In goal, the Leafs plucked 33 year old Johnny Bower from the minors and he was in the Toronto net for the next ten years. Defenseman

Right: Frank Mahovlich (27) puts the puck past sprawling Boston goalie Gerry Cheevers.

Allan Stanley was acquired from Boston and tough winger Bert Olmstead was claimed from Montreal. Perhaps Imlach's best deal was the trade that brought Red Kelly to Toronto. The Red Wings gave up on the all-star defender, letting him go to the Leafs for Marc Reaume. Imlach switched Kelly to center and put him on a line with a winger who could score, Frank Mahovlich. To play supporting roles Imlach picked up goalie Don Simmons, defensemen Al Arbour, Kent Douglas and Larry Hillman plus forwards like Ed Litzenberger, Gerry Ehman and Eddie Shack. These players provided the depth Toronto needed to become a winner.

Mahovlich was clearly Toronto's superstar. They had been grooming him since his days at St. Michael's High School. Big, strong and gifted with a great shot and superior skating skills, the "Big M" would lead the Leafs in the goal scoring department year after year. Other young Maple Leafs who rose to prominence were the swift skating Dave Keon, the rambunctious Carl Brewer and scoring wingers Bob Nevin and Dick Duff. These players joined other longer term Leafs like George Armstrong, Bob Baun, Billy Harris, Tim Horton, Bob Pulford and Ron Stewart. Imlach had a team poised to take a run at the Stanley Cup.

Toronto made a second straight appearance in the Finals in 1960 but lost to the powerful Canadiens one more time. In 1961, the Leafs made an early exit from the playoffs with a surprising loss to Detroit. However, in 1962 the Leafs were healthy and ready to win it all. They ousted the Rangers in six games and then played the defending champion Chicago Blackhawks for the Stanley Cup.

The teams split the first four games but Toronto won the fifth game 8 - 4, largely on the hat trick scored by Bob Pulford. Game six in Chicago was a classic Stanley Cup match. It was a 0 - 0 tie until 8:58 of the third when Bobby Hull scored to give the Blackhawks the lead. After a wild celebration by the Chicago crowd which lasted about ten minutes while the ice was cleared of debris, Bob Nevin quickly tied the score with a goal at 10:29.

The Leafs moved in for the kill with Tim Horton setting up Dick Duff for the winning goal at 14:14. With Don Simmons in goal the Leafs hung on and had their first Stanley Cup in eleven years.

The Leafs came back to finish on top of the NHL in 1962-63 for the first time since the 1947-48 season. In the playoffs, the Leafs knocked off the Canadiens in five, and Detroit also in five, to capture their second consecutive Cup. Toronto's third straight Cup was much more difficult to win. Imlach had to give up some young players including Dick Duff and Bob Nevin to obtain Andy Bathgate and Don McKenney in a late season deal with New York. The two new players gave the Leafs a much needed boost, and they won two hard fought seven game series over Montreal and Detroit.

The Toronto team was built around a disciplined defensive system. They were not as flashy as the Montreal Canadiens but the hard driving Imlach always had his team ready for the playoffs. Relying on the great goaltending of Johnny Bower and a feared defensive foursome (Horton, Stanley, Brewer, Baun), they also received clutch goal scoring from forwards like Keon, Armstrong and Pulford. It was a lethal combination that dominated the league during the Sixties.

The last great moment for this group of Leafs came in Canada's Centennial year, 1967. After disappointing playoff performances in 1965 and 1966, the Leafs pulled off two major upsets to win their fourth Stanley Cup of the decade. The 1967 team had a number of veterans well into their thirties. They also had some youngsters like Brian Conacher, Ron Ellis, Jim Pappin and Peter Stemkowski. Another key player was goalie Terry Sawchuk who the Leafs had picked up in 1965. Sawchuk and Bower combined to give the Leafs spectacular goaltending throughout the 1967 playoffs.

Toronto won game five of the Finals 4 - 1 at Montreal and returned home hoping to eliminate the Canadiens at Maple Leaf Gardens. It was a tense game throughout, but the Leafs held on to a 2 - 1 lead with less than a minute to go. With the Montreal goalie on the bench Imlach sent out his old vets to do the job in front of Sawchuk. Horton, Stanley, Pulford, Kelly and Armstrong handled the task with calmness and efficiency. They put a goal in the empty net to seal a 3 - 1 win.

It marked the end of a glorious era in Toronto Maple Leaf history!

Opposite: The heart of the stellar Toronto defense, goalie Johnny Bower (1), defensemen Allan Stanley (26) and Tim Horton (7).

GEORGE ARMSTRONG

George Armstrong was never a flashy player but while others left the game early, he played in the NHL for twenty-one seasons. Even Armstrong didn't think he would play that long, but he managed to develop a style that made him very valuable to the Toronto Maple Leafs.

Armstrong got a taste of winning early in his hockey career when the Toronto Marlies won the Memorial Cup. He followed with a senior hockey title (Allan Cup) and a Calder Cup with the Pittsburgh Hornets of the American Hockey League.

It was in Pittsburgh where Armstrong's role as a hockey player evolved. Somewhat awkward and not possessing great speed, Armstrong learned to play a tenacious two way game. He could stickhandle effectively and was known as a steady, positionally sound player who could be relied upon to contribute his share of goals.

*Above: Leaf captain George Armstrong battles Bruins'
defenseman Doug Mohns.*

*Opposite: Armstrong (10) is about to put the puck into
the open Montreal net vacated by Charlie Hodge (1).*

When he came to the Leafs, he displayed leadership abilities which led to his being named a captain of the team. He was the last appointed captain by Conn Smythe, the long-time owner and manager of the Toronto club. It proved to be an excellent choice as, under Armstrong's leadership, the Leafs won four Stanley Cups during the Sixties. He still holds the Toronto team record for most seasons and most games played. Armstrong was the modest type but there is no doubt he could be inspirational when it was necessary.

Called "Chief" because of his Indian ancestry, Armstrong coached the Toronto Marlies to two Memorial Cups. He later turned to scouting and briefly coached the Maple Leafs. He was elected to the Hall of Fame in 1975.

Born: 7-6-1930, Bowlands, Ontario
Height: 6'1"   Weight: 194   Shot: Right   Position: Right Wing
Sweater # 10   Years Played: 1949 - 1971
Teams: Toronto

	GP	G	A	PTS	PM
	1187	296	417	713	721
Playoffs:	110	26	34	60	88

BOBBY BAUN

The sixth game of the 1964 Finals between Toronto and Detroit was tied 3-3. The Toronto team needed a win to force a seventh game back at Maple Leaf Gardens while the Red Wings were trying to win their first championship since 1955. With about 10 minutes to go, Detroit's Gordie Howe took a shot which was blocked by Leaf defenseman Bobby Baun. However, the hard shot broke a bone in Baun's ankle. Carried out on a stretcher, it appeared Baun's season was over.

As the teams came out for the overtime period, Baun emerged with the rest of his teammates. Taking a shot of painkiller and taping his ankle very tightly, he managed to put his skate on despite the agony. After the first shift was done, Baun went on to the ice to take his regular turn. Suddenly, the puck was on Baun's stick at the Detroit blueline. He let a shot go toward the Detroit net. The puck hit Bill Gadsby's stick and went over Terry Sawchuk's shoulder giving the Leafs their much needed victory.

Nothing was going to keep Baun out of the seventh game. He refused to have doctors x-ray the ankle and showed up at the rink just before game time. He didn't miss a shift the entire game as the Leafs triumphed 4 - 0 and a third straight Stanley Cup victory.

"Boomer" Baun was one of the toughest defensemen ever to play in the NHL. His solid build allowed him to deliver a hard, clean bodycheck that could destroy an opponent. A good skater and shot blocker, Baun was paired with the

feisty Carl Brewer. It was a combination many forwards found difficult to beat. Baun also had a heavy shot from the point scoring a career high eight goals in 1959-60.

Drafted by the Oakland Seals in 1967, Baun also played for Detroit before returning to Toronto in 1970.

Above: Always strong in his own end ,Bobby Baun (21) takes the puck away from Chicago's Doug Mohns (2).

Opposite: Baun jumps into the rush for a shot at Montreal goalie Charlie Hodge (1).

Born: 9-9-1936, Lanigan, Saskatchewan
Height: 5'9" Weight: 182 Shot: Right Position: Defense
Sweater # 21   Years Played: 1956 - 1973
Teams: Toronto, Oakland, Detroit

	GP	G	A	PTS	PM
	964	37	187	224	1493
Playoffs:	96	3	12	15	171

JOHNNY BOWER

134

In 1958, the Maple Leafs decided they needed to find themselves a new goalie because Ed Chadwick's work was not to their liking. Leafs' coach Billy Reay first thought of one time Toronto netminder Al Rollins. After watching a poor performance by Rollins, Reay turned his attention to minor leaguer Johnny Bower. The Leafs drafted Bower from Cleveland of the American Hockey League. There was just one problem – Bower did not want to go to Toronto. He had his fill of the NHL in a stint with the New York Rangers and at the age of 33 he wasn't in the mood to move again.

Bower couldn't be faulted for being comfortable in the minors. He started his career in pro hockey in the 1945-46 season when he played 41 games with the Cleveland Barons of the AHL. He stayed there for eight straight years before playing the entire 1953-54 season with the Rangers. Despite a good year in New York, Bower found himself back in the minors replaced ironically enough, by the man he had beaten out for the job, Gump Worsley. Bower had every reason to believe his days in the NHL were over. The Leafs came calling and he had an important decision to make.

Luckily, the Leafs were able to convince Bower (with a two year contract) that he should give the big league one more try. He ended up playing more than ten years in Toronto enjoying a major role in four Stanley Cup wins. He added two Vezina Trophies (sharing one with Terry Sawchuk) and made the first all-star team in 1960-61.

During his years with Toronto he became known as "the ageless wonder" since his actual age was the topic of much speculation. Very competitive at all times, Bower took practice as serious as a game. The classic late bloomer, Bower's achievements were recognized with his induction to the Hall of Fame in 1976.

Below: Johnny Bower does the splits to stop the Blackhawk's Murray Balfour (8).

Opposite: Pulled out of the minor leagues in 1958, Bower backstopped the Leafs to four Stanley Cups.

Born: 11-8-1924, Prince Albert, Saskatchewan
Height: 5'11" Weight: 189 Shot: Left position: Goalie
Sweater # 1   Years Played: 1953 to 1970
Teams: New York, Toronto

	GP	W	L	T	AVG	SO
	549	251	196	90	2.52	37
Playoffs:	74	34	35	-	2.54	5

DICK DUFF

Dick Duff gained a well earned reputation as a money player. It started in the final game of the 1958-59 season. A win by Toronto would vault them ahead of New York and into the final playoff spot. The Leafs found themselves in a 4 - 4 tie in the third period against Detroit, when Leaf centre Larry Regan told Duff to be at an appointed spot on the ice. Duff followed the plan perfectly, Regan fed him the puck, and he whipped the puck home as the Leafs went on to win 6 - 4. The miracle Leafs of 1959 reached the Finals against Montreal but managed only one win on an overtime goal by none other than Dick Duff.

Three years later Duff scored the most memorable goal of his career against the Chicago Blackhawks in the sixth game of the 1962 Finals. The Leafs tied the score 1 - 1 in the third and pressed for the winner. Duff took a pass from Tim Horton, and using Dave Keon as a screen, put a

shot past goalie Glenn Hall. It was the Stanley Cup winning goal and marked the first for Toronto since 1951. In the first game of the 1963 Finals, Duff scored two goals after just 68 seconds of play. It set the tone for the series against Detroit and the Leafs won their second consecutive Cup easily.

Duff joined the Leafs right after his junior career ended with the Toronto Marlies. In only his second season with Toronto, Duff scored 26 goals after he had netted 18 as a rookie. In 1958-59 Duff enjoyed his best year with the Maple Leafs when he had 29 goals and 24 assists. He was included in a major deal that brought Andy Bathgate from New York to Toronto in 1964, but Duff could never find his game with the Rangers. Dealt to Montreal, Duff returned to form and made major contributions in four Montreal Stanley Cup wins between 1965 and 1969.

*Below: Dick Duff (9) tries to put the puck past
Boston goalie Bobby Perreault while being
checked by Jerry Toppazzini (21).*

*Opposite: Duff waits for a loose puck around
Montreal goalie Jacques Plante.*

Born: 2-18-1936, Kirkland Lake, Ontario
Height: 5'9"   Weight: 166   Shot: Left   Position: Left Wing
Sweater # 9   Years Played: 1954 - 1972
Teams: Toronto, NY Rangers, Montreal, Los Angeles, Buffalo

	GP	G	A	PTS	PM
	1030	283	286	569	774
Playoffs:	114	30	49	79	78

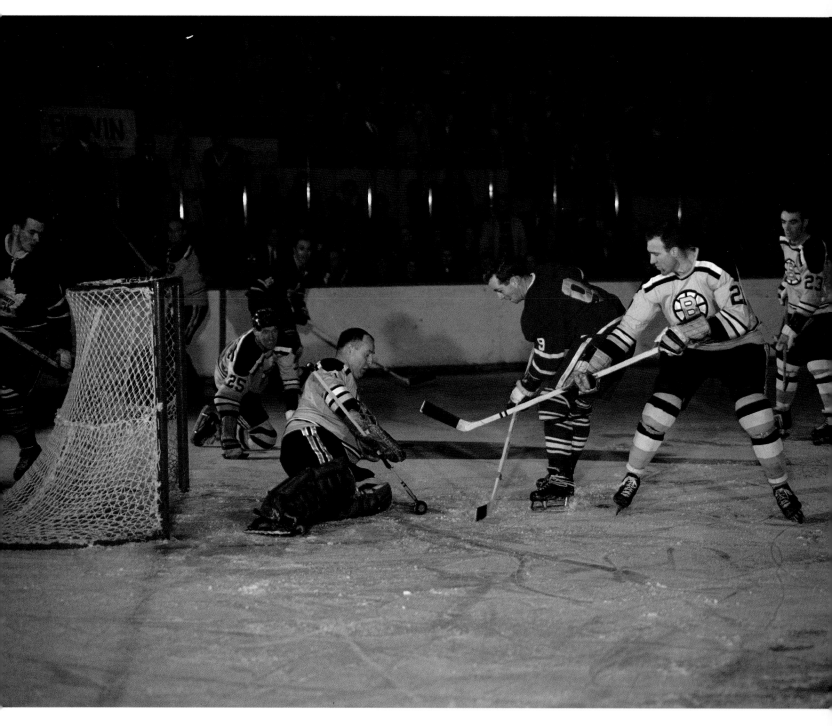

TIM HORTON

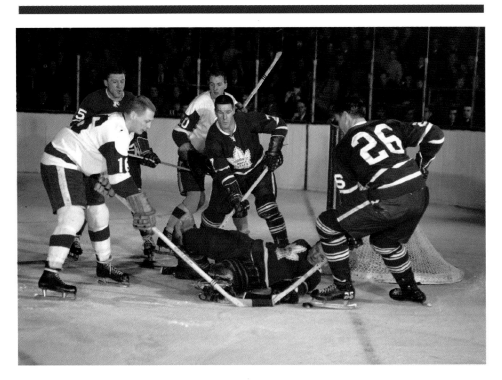

It took a long time for Tim Horton to achieve stardom as an NHL defenseman. He joined the Toronto Maple Leafs at the tender age of 22, but outlasted many other players he started with, such as Leo Boivin, Fern Flaman, Marc Reaume, Jim Morrison and Hugh Bolton. The coaches came and went but Horton hung around.

In March, 1955 Horton received a devastating bodycheck by Bill Gadsby of the New York Rangers that broke his leg and jaw. It was unknown if he could resume his career with any kind of effectiveness. Gradually, both Horton and the team started to get better.

As he gained confidence, Horton started to rush the puck the length of the rink and would unleash a low hard shot from the point. The Leafs saw their patience really pay off during the 1962 playoffs when Horton set a new mark for defenseman as he contributed 16 points to the Leafs' Stanley Cup victory. In 1963-64, Horton was the only non-Blackhawk to make the first all-star team. Ironically, he would not make the first team again until the Leafs fell out of contention in 1967-68 and 1968-69. He was a durable performer and played in 461 consecutive games for the Leafs which is still a club record.

With a bull-like build, Horton's physical strength was legendary. When upset, Horton was known to toss bodies around or apply a bear hug until the opponent almost had the life squeezed out of him. Fortunately, Horton held his temper in line for of the time.

A rebuilding Leaf team traded him to New York in 1970, and he later played with Pittsburgh and Buffalo. He played his final game at Maple Leaf Gardens in 1973 while with the Sabres, and was named one of the three stars despite playing in only two periods.

Born: 1-12-1930, Cochrane, Ontario					
Height: 5'10" Weight: 180 Shot: Right Position: Defense					
Sweater # 7 Years Played: 1949 - 1974					
Teams: Toronto, NY Rangers, Pittsburgh, Buffalo					
	GP	G	A	PTS	PM
	1446	115	403	518	1611
Playoffs:	126	11	39	50	183

Opposite: Tim Horton was good at leading the rush out of his own end like he does here against Chicago.

Above: In the middle of the action, Horton (7) helps out Johnny Bower and Allan Stanley (26) fight off a Detroit attack.

RED KELLY

Toronto general manager Punch Imlach made many shrewd moves as he built the Maple Leafs into a powerhouse that won four Stanley Cups in seven years. Perhaps his most important and successful deal was acquiring Leonard "Red" Kelly from Detroit in 1960. The Red Wings had actually sent Kelly to the New York Rangers in another deal but he refused to report saying he would rather retire. Imlach sensed an opportunity and after getting Kelly to agree to come to Toronto, he offered Detroit defenseman Marc Reaume. The Red Wings

agreed and the Leafs began to enjoy the benefits of one of their greatest deals.

The Red Wings displeasure with Kelly had to be considered a surprise. When Kelly joined the Red Wings as a defenseman in 1947 their fortunes began to rise. As one of the first rear-guards to lead rushes down the ice, he helped Detroit to seven first place finishes and four Stanley Cup wins. Kelly's dominance on the blueline was evidenced by the fact that he made the first all-star team six times. In 1953-54, Red Kelly was named as the first

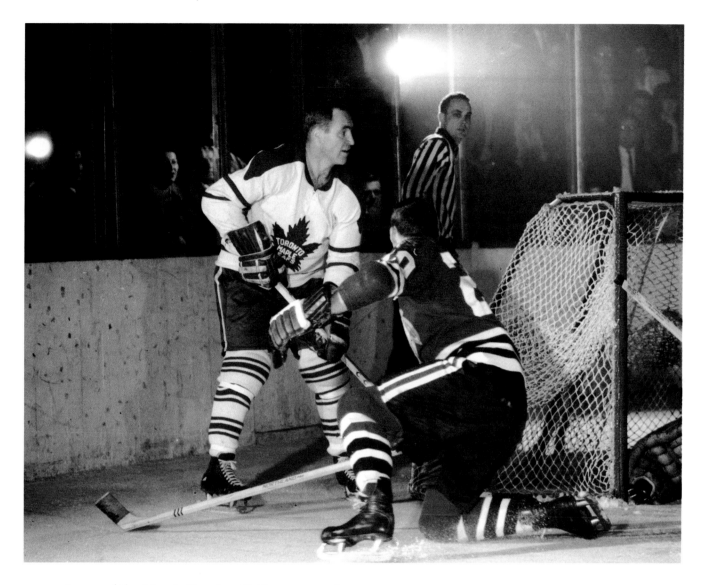

ever winner of the Norris Trophy. Kelly was good at generating offence but he was more than capable in his own end without taking needless penalties. He won the Lady Byng three times. No defenseman has won that award since.

Kelly was also versatile.In Toronto, Imlach moved Kelly to center, and it is generally recognized that he revived slumping winger Frank Mahovlich. Moving a superstar to a new position was a rarity, but Kelly was a good checker and could thread passes to spring the "Big M" down the wing.The four championships in Toronto gave Kelly a total of eight – unusual for a player who did not play for the Montreal Canadiens.

Off the ice Kelly was busy as a Member of Parliament in Ottawa for two terms while he played for the Leafs. He gave up his political career to concentrate on hockey and later tried his hand at coaching Los Angeles, Pittsburgh and finally with Toronto between 1973 and 1977.

Opposite: Leafs' Red Kelly (4) scores on Boston goalie Bobby Perreault (1) with Ted Green (6) and Leo Boivin (20) unable to help.

Above: Kelly looks to use his playmaking skills from behind the net.

Born: 7-9-1927, Simcoe, Ontario					
Height: 6' Weight: 195 Shot: Left Position: Center					
Sweater # 4 Years Played: 1947 - 1967					
Teams: Detroit, Toronto					
	GP	G	A	PTS	PM
	1316	281	542	823	327
Playoffs:	164	33	59	92	51

DAVE KEON

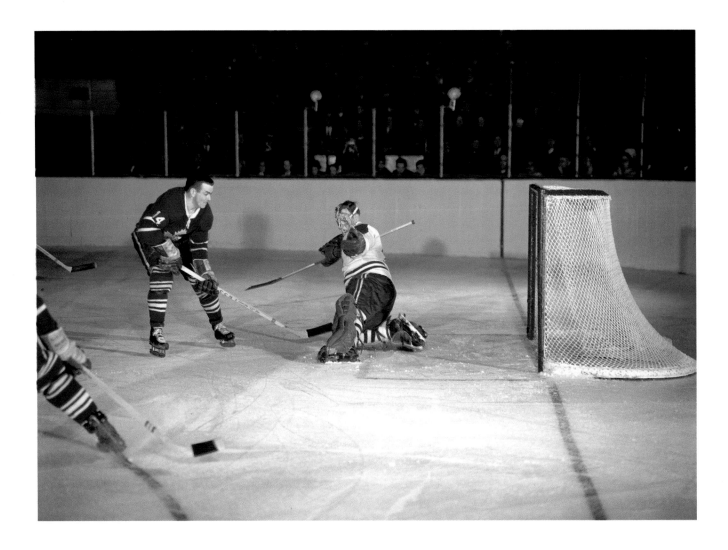

The Toronto scout in Quebec wrote a letter to the Maple Leafs urging them to sign a young man from Noranda, adding that they might regret it one day if they did not. The Leafs heeded the advice and were able to convince Dave Keon that he should take a hockey scholarship to St. Michael's High School in Toronto. While at St. Mike's, Keon was coached by the renowned mentor of the Canadian Olympic hockey team, Father David Bauer, who taught Keon an effective checking method for a player of his small stature. Keon learned his lessons well as his tenacious checking abilities became his NHL trademark.

Keon was not expected to make the Leafs at his first training camp. Fearing that he might be too small to play in the NHL, Keon was ticketed for Rochester to get some seasoning. But during a west coast exhibition tour, Keon played himself onto the team and never looked back. He won the Calder Trophy in 1960-61 with 20 goals and 25 assists. He added the Lady Byng in both 1961-62 and 1962-63 when he had only two minutes in penalties in each of those seasons.

Although he played in a gentlemanly way, Keon was always very intense and responded to the pressure of big games. In a March, 1963 game against the Canadiens, Keon's goal with eight seconds left tied the game at 3 - 3 and gave Toronto a first place finish for the 1962-63 season. During the seventh game of the 1964 Semi-Finals against Montreal, Keon scored all three goals in a 3 - 1 Leaf win. The victory allowed Toronto to go on and complete the Stanley Cup hat trick.

Perhaps his greatest moment came in the 1967 playoffs when he won the Conn Smythe Trophy after a tireless skating and checking performance against Chicago and Montreal. A gifted skater with a whirling style and great speed, Keon used his abilities to become a top penalty killer. He showed great desire in every game and set a fine example for his teammates. Keon was named captain of the Leafs in 1969.

Born: 3-22-1940, Noranda, Quebec				
Height: 5'9" Weight: 167 Shot: Left Position: Center				
Sweater # 14 Years Played:1960 - 1982				
Teams: Toronto, Hartford				
GP	G	A	PTS	PM
1296	396	590	986	117
Playoffs: 92	32	36	68	6

Opposite: Dave Keon (14) tries to put a shot behind Montreal goalie Charlie Hodge.

Below: Keon has a great chance to score with Detroit's Terry Sawchuk down on the ice.

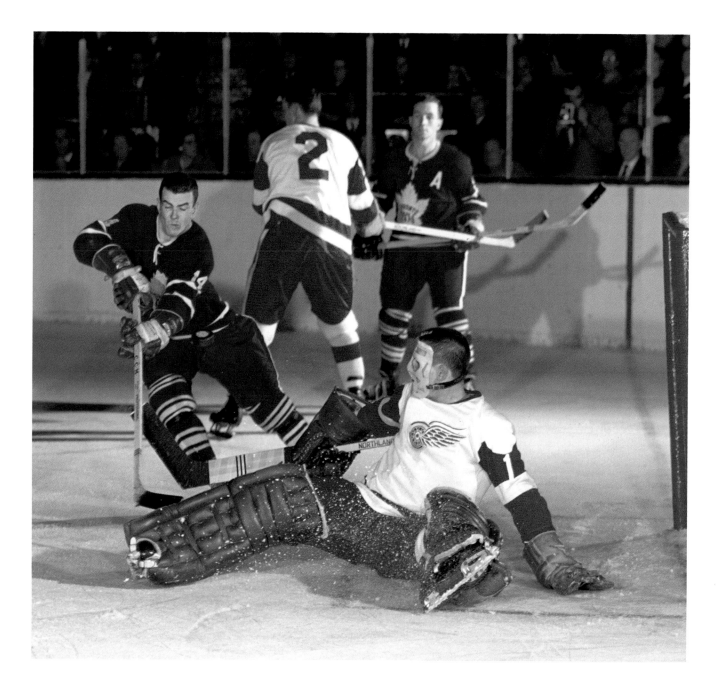

FRANK MAHOVLICH

Imagine what a million dollars meant in the early Sixties. In October, 1962 the Chicago Blackhawks offered the Toronto Maple Leafs that precise sum of money for the services of winger Frank Mahovlich. The Hawks presented the Leafs with a cheque and dreamed of having the best two left wingers in the NHL (Bobby Hull being the other) playing on the same team. When word of the deal leaked out, it wiped the baseball World Series off the front pages. The million dollar cheque represented the largest offer ever made for a professional athlete. It may have been tempting but the Leafs turned down the offer and kept the "Big M."

The Toronto club knew of Mahovlich's true value going all the way back to minor hockey. Leafs' scout Bob Davidson convinced Mahovlich to attend St. Michael's High School in Toronto. He starred in the OHA and was named the league's best player for 1956-57. He turned pro the following year with the Leafs and as a rookie playing for a last place team scored 20 goals and 16 assists. He was awarded the Calder Trophy by edging out Bobby Hull in the voting. Three years later, in 1960-61, Mahovlich scored 48 goals which stood as a team record for the next 21 years. He led the Leafs in goals scored for six consecutive years between 1961 and 1966.

Mahovlich's physical attributes were a sight to behold when in full flight. He skated with an easy,

fluid stride and made good use of his long reach, strength and laser like shot. He showed an ability to run over the opposition, especially defensemen who were in his way when he wanted to drive to the net. It was unfortunate that a rather critical Toronto public always expected Mahovlich to play like a superstar on the rampage.

After ten years and four Stanley Cups with Toronto, the Leafs dealt him to Detroit where he flourished under a little less pressure. He scored 49 goals with Detroit and when he was traded to Montreal, Mahovlich added two more Stanley Cup rings to his collection.

	GP	G	A	PTS	PM
	1181	533	570	1103	1056
Playoffs:	137	51	67	118	163

Born: 1-10-1938, Timmins, Ontario
Height: 6' Weight: 205 Shot; Left Position: Left Wing
Sweater # 27 Years Played: 1956 - 1974
Teams: Toronto, Detroit, Montreal

Above: Frank Mahovlich was a sight to behold when he was winding up for a rush down the ice.

Opposite: Mahovlich uses his size and strength to control the puck against Boston's Ted Green (6).

BOB PULFORD

Some players just have a knack of scoring important goals. Bob Pulford was one such player for the Maple Leafs. He first started this trend in March, 1959 when the Leafs were desperately chasing the New York Rangers for the final playoff spot. In the second half of a key weekend series, Pulford scored a late goal to give Toronto a 6 - 5 win and a two game sweep. Toronto eventually passed the Rangers by a single point to earn a berth in post season action.

In the 1962 Finals against Chicago, the Leafs were at home for the fifth game after the Blackhawks had tied the series with two straight wins at home. The Hawks appeared to have the momentum

needed to capture their second consecutive championship. However, Pulford poured in three goals past Glenn Hall in a 8 - 4 Toronto win. It shifted the tide back to the Leafs who won the Stanley Cup with a victory in the next game.

Pulford's next clutch goal came in the first game of the 1964 Finals against Detroit. With the score tied 2 - 2 and the Leafs shorthanded, Pulford stole the puck at his own blueline, broke away from Gordie Howe, and lifted a backhand shot over Terry Sawchuk. There were only two seconds left to play in the third period! Toronto went on to capture their third consecutive Stanley Cup.

Pulford's sense for drama was not yet complete. In the 1967 Finals gainst the favoured Canadiens, Pulford scored in the second overtime period of the third game giving Toronto a vital 2 - 1 series lead which they would win in six.

Pulford's heroics should not be considered as much of a surprise. He was an honest hockey player who worked very hard at shutting down the opposition's top players.His forechecking and physically abrasive style put him in great position to score timely goals. He was often in great demand in trade talks, but the Leafs only let him go well past him prime in 1970. He was dealt to the Los Angeles Kings where he was named captain.

Below: Bob Pulford (20) moves in on Detroit's Terry Sawchuk (1) while Marcel Pronovost (3) tries to hold him back.

Opposite: Pulford clashes with Boston's Ted Green.

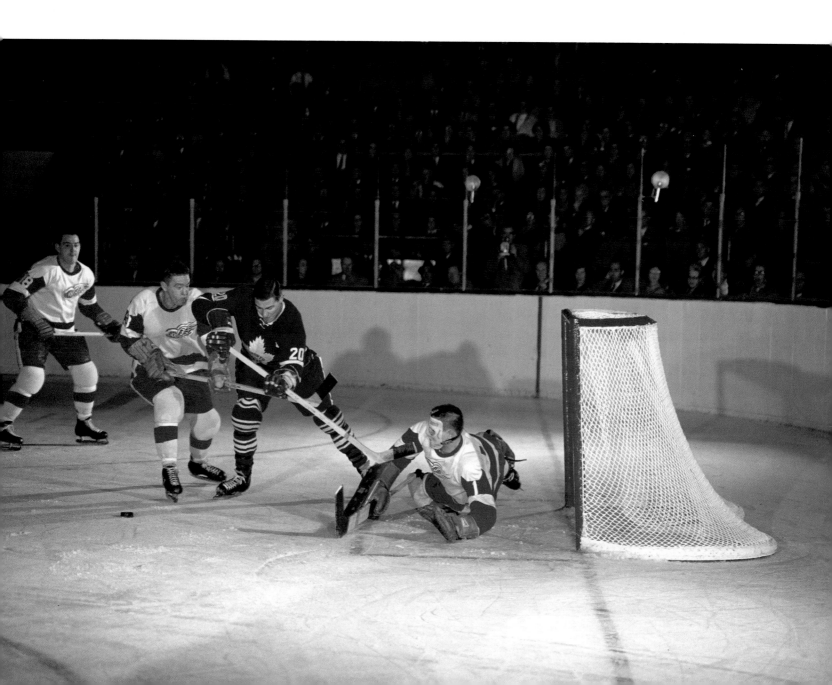

CARL BREWER

Above: Carl Brewer (2) defends against Detroit's Floyd Smith.

If there is one word to describe Carl Brewer, it has to be unpredictable. In 1965, Brewer, then 26 and at the prime of his career, decided to walk out and retire from hockey. It was well known that Brewer had his disagreements with coach Punch Imlach, but his sudden decision to leave the game caught everyone by surprise.

Brewer joined the Leafs in 1958 and was teamed with Bobby Baun to form a strong pair at the blueline. Brewer played an aggressive brand of hockey which unfortunately resulted in his twice leading the NHL in penalty minutes. A swift skater who could jump into the attack, Brewer was named to the first all-star team in 1962-63.

After leaving the Leafs, Brewer was reinstated as an amateur which allowed him to play for the Canadian National Team in 1966-67. He returned to the NHL with Detroit in the 1967-68 season and recorded a career high 37 assists before he was sent on to St. Louis.

In 1980, Brewer pulled another shocker by coming out of a long retirement to play for Punch Imlach and the Maple Leafs!

Born: 10-21-1938, Toronto, Ontario
Height: 5'10" Weight: 180 Shot: Left Position: Defense
Sweater # 2   Years Played: 1957 - 1980
Teams: Toronto, Detroit, St. Louis

	GP	G	A	PTS	PM
	604	25	198	223	1037
Playoffs:	72	3	17	20	146

RON ELLIS

Above: Leafs' Ron Ellis (11) was often assigned to check Blackhawks' Bobby Hull.

Ron Ellis played on some very notable winning teams during his hockey career. In junior, Ellis played for the Memorial Cup champion Toronto Marlboros in 1964. It was called one of the greatest junior clubs of all-time. In 1967, Ellis was a youngster on a team of aging veterans as the Maple Leafs won a surprising Stanley Cup. Finally, in 1972, Ellis played a key checking role on Team Canada as they battled back to beat the Russian National Team in the Summit Series.

The strongest part of the rightwinger's game was his skating, although his heavy shot allowed him to score a few goals as is evidenced by the 64 he potted while playing for the Marlies. When Ellis made it to the Leafs he established himself as a good two-way player. In his rookie year he scored 23 goals and finished second to Roger Crozier in the Calder Trophy voting.

Ellis retired in 1981 after more than 1,000 games as a Maple Leaf.

		Born: 1-8-1945, Lindsay, Ontario			
	Height: 5'9" Weight: 195 Shot: Right Position: Right Wing				
		Sweater # 6 Years Played: 1963 - 1981			
		Teams: Toronto			
	GP	**G**	**A**	**PTS**	**PM**
	1034	332	308	640	207
Playoffs:	70	18	8	26	20

BERT OLMSTEAD

Above: A tough competitor, Bert Olmstead holds his ground against Boston's Leo Boivin.

A very tough and determined player, Bert Olmstead always played the game with a physical gusto. He was especially good in the corners where he worked fearlessly. Once he had the puck, he could make accurate passes to teammates in front of the goal. Twice he led the NHL in assists and had 421 over his career. He didn't score many goals, but his work was certainly appreciated by the teams he played on. He could make short work of any opponent who dared to challenge him. It was this type of attitude that made Olmstead a leader.

Olmstead started his career in Chicago, but he was dealt to Detroit before being sent to the Montreal Canadiens. With Montreal he often played with Maurice Richard who benefited from Olmstead set-ups from the corners. After four

Stanley Cups in Montreal, the Maple Leafs took him in the intra-league draft where he stayed until the Toronto triumph of 1962. He could have kept playing but decided to retire.

In 1967 Olmstead became the first coach of the expansion Oakland Seals.

Born: 9-4-1926, Scepter, Saskatchewan
Height: 6'2" Weight: 183 Shot: Left Position: Left Wing
Sweater # 16 Years Played:1948 - 1962
Teams: Chicago, Montreal, Toronto

	GP	G	A	PTS	PM
	848	181	421	602	874
Playoffs:	115	16	42	58	101

EDDIE SHACK

Above: Eddie Shack (23) waits for a pass while Rangers' Jim Neilson (15) moves in.

Eddie Shack's hockey career started in the New York Rangers' junior system with the Guelph Biltmores where he scored 47 goals and 57 assists for 104 points in his final season. It created an air of expectation for Shack's arrival in New York. His NHL debut was anticipated even more eagerly as he developed a reputation for being a tough customer. But when Shack joined the Rangers in 1958-59 he had difficulties with the coach, and was dealt to Toronto in November, 1960.

It was while Shack played for the Leafs that "The Entertainer" was born. When he took the ice there was never a dull moment. After gathering speed, he would swirl, catapult and fling himself at the opposition. His reckless style brought a certain energy to the game. Nobody, including Shack, knew what he was going to do next. His style was very popular with the fans and a "we want Shack" chant would reverberate throughout the Gardens.

He also had a song written about him called "Clear The Track, Here Comes Shack." It made the top of the charts in Toronto.

Shack responded by playing hard every shift and chipping in with a few goals. He shared in all the Toronto Stanley Cup wins in the Sixties and even scored the winning goal in the 1963 Finals against Detroit.

Born: 2-11-1937, Sudbury, Ontario
Height: 6'1" Weight: 200 Shot: Left Position: Right Wing
Sweater # 23   Years Played: 1958 - 1975
Teams: New York Rangers, Toronto, Boston
Los Angeles, Buffalo, Pittsburgh

	GP	G	A	PTS	PM
	1047	239	226	465	1437
Playoffs:	74	6	7	13	151

ALLAN STANLEY

Above: Allan Stanley moves in on the Montreal net hoping Canadiens' defenseman Jean Guy Talbot (17) will make a mistake.

There were great expectations of Allan Stanley when the New York Rangers acquired him in 1948. He was a defenseman with the tools to be an all-star for many years. He played an efficient but unspectacular brand of defense, and it was this style which led Stanley to fall into disfavour with the New York fans.

By 1954, the Rangers had seen enough and traded him to Chicago. Two years later, Chicago sent him to Boston, who then traded him to the Maple Leafs in 1958. Most hockey observers thought it was all over for the veteran. But in Toronto, he found himself paired with Tim Horton and on a team that was suddenly on the rise.

With the Leafs, Stanley made the second all-star team twice and helped anchor a Leaf defense that won four Stanley Cups. The man they called "Snowshoes" because of the way he skated, also became quite capable at carrying the puck out of his own end.

In the final moments of the 1967 Finals against Montreal, it was Stanley who was designated by Leaf coach Punch Imlach to take a key face-off against Jean Beliveau. Stanley won the draw and the Leafs scored into an empty net to clinch a 3 - 1 win. It capped a remarkable comeback for the career of Allan Stanley.

Born: 3-1-1926, Timmins, Ontario
Height: 6'2" Weight: 191 Shot: Left Position: Defense
Sweater # 26 Years Played: 1948 - 1969
Teams: New York Rangers, Chicago, Boston, Toronto, Philadelphia

	GP	G	A	PTS	PM
	1244	100	333	433	792
Playoffs:	109	7	36	43	80

RON STEWART

Above: Ron Stewart (12) has good position on Montreal's Henri Richard.

Born in Calgary, Ron Stewart decided he needed to come East if he was going to be serious about his hockey career. At 16 years of age, he moved to Toronto and caught on with the junior Marlboros.

The Toronto Maple Leafs invited him to attend the camp of their top farm team in Pittsburgh, but an injury to George Armstrong gave Stewart a chance with the big team. He quickly found himself playing with legendary Leafs' Ted Kennedy and Sid Smith. Stewart's good play earned him a spot on the team ahead of the more highly touted Eric Nesterenko. Stewart had made the NHL without playing a single game in the minors. He played in all 70 games in 1952-53 adding 13 goals and 22 assists.

An effortless and smooth skater, Stewart developed a role as a checker. Stewart's defensive niche helped him to stay around because he was never a prolific goal scorer. In his 21 NHL seasons,

Stewart never scored more than 21 goals in a single season. His highest point production was 39 with Toronto in 1957-58. Stewart could also play on defense if necessary.

A part of three consecutive Leaf Cup wins, Stewart played in the 1962 playoffs with cracked ribs he received in an auto accident. He was still able to contribute a goal and six assists in 11 games.

	Born: 7-11-1932, Calgary, Alberta				
	Height: 6'1" Weight: 197 Shot: Right Position: Right Wing				
	Sweater # 12 Years Played: 1952 - 1973				
	Teams: Toronto, Boston, St. Louis, NY Rangers,				
	Vancouver, NY Islanders				
	GP	G	A	PTS	PM
	1353	276	253	529	560
Playoffs:	119	14	21	35	60

RECORDS AND AWARDS
(1957 - 1967)

*NHL Trophies of the Golden Era, clockwise from left: the Calder, the Hart, the Wales, the Stanley Cup,
the George Vezina, the Lady Byng, the James Norris, the Art Ross (foreground).*

1957-58

FINAL STANDINGS

	W	L	T	PTS
Montreal	43	17	10	96
New York	32	25	13	77
Detroit	29	29	12	70
Boston	27	28	15	69
Chicago	24	39	7	55
Toronto	21	38	11	53

LEADING SCORERS

	G	A	PTS	
Dickie Moore, Mon.	36	48	84	(Art Ross)
Henri Richard, Mon.	28	52	80	
Andy Bathgate, N.Y.	30	48	78	
Gordie Howe, Det.	33	48	78	
Bronco Horvath, Bos.	30	36	66	

1958-59

FINAL STANDINGS

	W	L	T	PTS
Montreal	39	18	13	91
Boston	32	29	9	73
Chicago	28	29	13	69
Toronto	27	32	11	65
New York	26	32	12	64
Detroit	25	37	8	58

LEADING SCORERS

	G	A	PTS	
Dickie Moore, Mon.	41	55	96	(Art Ross)
Jean Beliveau, Mon.	45	46	91	
Andy Bathgate, N.Y.	40	48	88	
Gordie Howe, Det.	32	46	78	
Ed Litzenberger, Chi.	33	44	77	

Most Penalty Minutes: Lou Fontinato, N.Y. 152
Best Goal Against Avg: Jacques Plante, Mon. 2.11 (Vezina)
Most Shutouts: Jacques Plante, Mon. 9

Most Penalty Minutes: Ted Lindsay, Chi. 184
Best Goals Against Avg: Jacques Plante, Mon. 2.16 (Vezina)
Most Shutouts: Jacques Plante, Mon. 9

ALL-STAR TEAMS

	1st Team	2nd Team
Goal:	Glenn Hall, Chi.	Jacques Plante, Mon.
Defense:	Doug Harvey, Mon.	Fernie Flaman, Bos.
Defense:	Bill Gadsby, N.Y.	Marcel Pronovost, Det.
Center:	Henri Richard, Mon.	Jean Beliveau, Mon.
Left Wing:	Dickie Moore, Mon.	Camille Henry, N.Y.
Right Wing:	Gordie Howe, Det.	Andy Bathgate, N.Y.

ALL-STAR TEAMS

	1st Team	2nd Team
Goal:	Jacques Plante, Mon.	Terry Sawchuk, Det.
Defense:	Tom Johnson, Mon.	Marcel Pronovost, Det.
Defense:	Bill Gadsby, N.Y.	Doug Harvey, Mon.
Center:	Jean Beliveau, Mon.	Henri Richard, Mon.
Left Wing:	Dickie Moore, Mon.	Alex Delvecchio, Det.
Right Wing:	Andy Bathgate, N.Y.	Gordie Howe, Det.

AWARDS

Hart Trophy — Gordie Howe, Det.
Lady Byng Trophy — Camille Henry, N.Y.
Norris Trophy — Doug Harvey, Mon.
Calder Trophy — Frank Mahovlich, Tor.

AWARDS

Hart Trophy — Andy Bathgate, N.Y.
Lady Byng Trophy — Alex Delvecchio, Det.
Norris Trophy — Tom Johnson, Mon.
Calder Trophy — Ralph Backstrom, Mon.

PLAYOFF RESULTS

Semi-Finals:	Montreal over Detroit,	4 games to 0
	Boston over New York,	4 games to 2
Finals:	Montreal over Boston,	4 games to 2

Stanley Cup Winning Goal: Bernie Geoffrion, Mon.

PLAYOFF RESULTS

Semi-Finals:	Montreal over Chicago,	4 games to 2
	Toronto over Boston,	4 games to 3
Finals:	Montreal over Toronto,	4 games to 1

Stanley Cup Winning Goal: Marcel Bonin, Mon.

1959-60

FINAL STANDINGS

	W	L	T	PTS
Montreal	40	18	12	92
Toronto	35	26	9	79
Chicago	28	29	13	69
Detroit	26	29	15	67
Boston	28	34	8	64
New York	17	38	15	49

LEADING SCORERS

	G	A	PTS	
Bobby Hull, Chi.	39	42	81	(Art Ross)
Bronco Horvath, Bos.	39	41	80	
Jean Beliveau, Mon.	34	40	74	
Andy Bathgate, N.Y.	26	48	74	
Henri Richard, Mon.	30	43	73	

Most Penalty Minutes: Carl Brewer, Tor. 150
Best Goals Against Avg: Jacques Plante, Mon. 2.54 (Vezina)
Most Shutouts: Glenn Hall, Chi. 6

1960-61

FINAL STANDINGS

	W	L	T	PTS
Montreal	41	19	10	92
Toronto	39	19	12	90
Chicago	29	24	17	75
Detroit	25	29	16	66
New York	22	38	10	54
Boston	15	42	13	43

LEADING SCORERS

	G	A	PTS
Bernie Geoffrion, Mon.	50	45	95 (Art Ross)
Jean Beliveau, Mon.	32	58	90
Frank Mahovlich, Tor.	48	36	84
Andy Bathgate, N.Y.	29	48	77
Gordie Howe, Det.	23	49	72

Most Penalty Minutes: Pierre Pilote, Chi. 165
Best Goals Against Avg: Johnny Bower, Tor. 2.50 (Vezina)
Most Shutouts: Glenn Hall, Chi. 6

ALL-STAR TEAMS

	1st Team	2nd Team
Goal:	Glenn Hall, Chi.	Jacques Plante, Mon.
Defense:	Doug Harvey, Mon.	Allan Stanley, Tor.
Defense:	Marcel Pronovost, Det.	Pierre Pilote, Chi.
Center:	Jean Beliveau, Mon.	Bronco Horvath, Bos.
Left Wing:	Bobby Hull, Chi.	Dean Prentice, N.Y.
Right Wing:	Gordie Howe, Det.	Bernie Geoffrion, Mon.

AWARDS

Hart Trophy — Gordie Howe, Det.
Lady Byng Trophy — Don McKenney, Bos.
Norris Trophy — Doug Harvey, Mon.
Calder Trophy— Bill Hay, Chi.

PLAYOFF RESULTS

Semi-Finals:	Montreal over Chicago,	4 games to 0
	Toronto over Detroit,	4 games to 2
Finals:	Montreal over Toronto,	4 games to 0

Stanley Cup Winning Goal: Jean Beliveau, Mon.

ALL-STAR TEAMS

	1st Team	2nd Team
Goal:	Johnny Bower, Tor.	Glenn Hall, Chi.
Defense:	Doug Harvey, Mon.	Allan Stanley, Tor.
Defense:	Marcel Pronovost, Det.	Pierre Pilote, Chi.
Center:	Jean Beliveau, Mon.	Henri Richard, Mon.
Left Wing:	Frank Mahovlich, Tor.	Dickie Moore, Mon.
Right Wing:	Bernie Geoffrion, Mon.	Gordie Howe, Det.

AWARDS

Hart Trophy — Bernie Geoffrion, Mon.
Lady Byng Trophy — Red Kelly, Tor.
Norris Trophy — Doug Harvey, Mon.
Calder Trophy — Dave Keon, Tor.

PLAYOFFS RESULTS

Semi-Finals:	Chicago over Montreal,	4 games to 2
	Detroit over Toronto,	4 games to 1
Finals:	Chicago over Detroit,	4 games to 1

Stanley Cup Winning Goal: Ab McDonald, Chi.

1961-62

FINAL STANDINGS

	W	L	T	PTS
Montreal	42	14	14	98
Toronto	37	22	11	85
Chicago	31	26	13	75
New York	26	32	12	64
Detroit	23	33	14	60
Boston	15	47	8	38

LEADING SCORERS

	G	A	PTS
Bobby Hull, Chi.	50	34	84 (Art Ross)
Andy Bathgate, N.Y.	28	56	84
Gordie Howe, Det.	33	44	77
Stan Mikita, Chi.	25	52	77
Frank Mahovlich, Tor.	33	38	71

Most Penalty Minutes:	Lou Fontinato, Mon. 167
Best Goals Against Avg:	Jacques Plante, Mon. 2.37 (Vezina)
Most Shutouts:	Glenn Hall, Chi. 5

ALL-STAR TEAMS

	1st Team	2nd Team
Goal:	Jacques Plante, Mon.	Glenn Hall, Chi.
Defense:	Doug Harvey, N.Y.	Carl Brewer, Chi.
Defense:	Jean-Guy Talbot, Mon.	Pierre Pilote, Chi.
Defense:	Stan Mikita, Chi.	Dave Keon, Tor.
Left Wing:	Bobby Hull, Chi.	Frank Mahovlich, Tor.
Right Wing:	Andy Bathgate, N.Y.	Gordie Howe, Det.

1962-63

FINAL STANDINGS

	W	L	T	PTS
Toronto	35	23	12	82
Chicago	32	21	17	81
Montreal	28	19	23	79
Detroit	32	25	13	77
New York	22	36	12	56
Boston	14	39	17	45

LEADING SCORERS

	G	A	PTS
Gordie Howe, Det.	38	48	86 (Art Ross)
Andy Bathgate, N.Y.	35	46	81
Stan Mikita, Chi.	31	45	76
Frank Mahovlich, Tor.	36	37	73
Henri Richard, Mon.	23	50	73

Most Penalty Minutes:	Howie Young, Det. 273
Best Goals Against Avg:	Terry Sawchuk, Det. 2.48
Most Shutouts:	Jacques Plante, Mon. 5

ALL-STAR TEAMS

	1st Team	2nd Team
Goal:	Glenn Hall, Chi.	Terry Sawchuk, Det.
Defense:	Pierre Pilote, Chi.	Tim Horton, Tor.
Defense:	Carl Brewer, Tor.	Elmer Vasko, Chi.
Center:	Stan Mikita, Chi.	Henri Richard, Mon.
Left Wing:	Frank Mahovlich, Tor.	Bobby Hull, Chi.
Right Wing:	Gordie Howe, Det.	Andy Bathgate, N.Y.

1961-62 Continued

AWARDS

Hart Trophy — Jacques Plante, Mon.
Lady Byng Trophy — Dave Keon, Tor.
Norris Trophy — Doug Harvey, N.Y.
Calder Trophy — Bobby Rousseau, Mon.
Vezina Trophy — Jacques Plante, Mon.

PLAYOFF RESULTS

Semi-Finals:	Toronto over New York,	4 games to 2
	Chicago over Montreal,	4 games to 2
Finals:	Toronto over Chicago,	4 games to 2

Stanley Cup Winning Goal: Dick Duff, Tor.

1962-63 Continued

AWARDS

Hart Trophy — Gordie Howe, Det.
Lady Byng Trophy — Dave Keon, Tor.
Norris Trophy — Pierre Pilote, Chi.
Calder Trophy — Kent Douglas, Tor.
Vezina Trophy — Glenn Hall, Chi.

PLAYOFF RESULTS

Semi-Finals:	Toronto over Montreal,	4 games to 1
	Detroit over Chicago,	4 games to 2
Finals:	Toronto over Detroit,	4 games to 1

Stanley Cup Winning Goal: Eddie Shack, Tor.

Above: Toronto's George Armstrong holds hockey's most sought-after prize, the Stanley Cup, in 1967.

1963-64

FINAL STANDINGS

	W	L	T	PTS
Montreal	36	21	13	85
Chicago	36	22	12	84
Toronto	33	25	12	78
Detroit	30	29	11	71
New York	22	38	10	54
Boston	18	40	12	48

LEADING SCORERS

	G	A	PTS	
Stan Mikita, Chi.	39	50	89	(Art Ross)
Bobby Hull, Chi.	43	44	87	
Jean Beliveau, Mon.	28	50	78	
Andy Bathgate, N.Y./Tor.	19	58	77	
Gordie Howe, Det.	26	47	73	

Most Penalty Minutes:	Vic Hadfield, N.Y.	151
Best Goals Against Avg:	Johnny Bower, Tor.	2.11
Most Shutouts:	Charlie Hodge, Mon.	8

1964-65

FINAL STANDINGS

	W	L	T	PTS
Detroit	40	23	7	87
Montreal	36	23	11	83
Chicago	34	28	8	76
Toronto	30	26	14	74
New York	20	38	12	52
Boston	21	43	6	48

LEADING SCORERS

	G	A	PTS	
Stan Mikita, Chi.	28	59	87	(Art Ross)
Norm Ullman, Det.	42	41	83	
Gordie Howe, Det.	29	47	76	
Bobby Hull, Chi.	39	32	71	
Alex Delvecchio, Det.	25	42	67	

Most Penalty Minutes:	Carl Brewer, Tor.	177
Best Goals Against Avg:	Johnny Bower, Tor.	2.38
Most Shutouts:	Roger Crozier, Det.	6

ALL-STAR TEAMS

	1st Team	2nd Team
Goal:	Glenn Hall, Chi.	Charlie Hodge, Mon.
Defense:	Pierre Pilote, Chi.	Elmer Vasko, Chi.
Defense:	Tim Horton, Tor.	J. Laperriere, Mon.
Center:	Stan Mikita, Chi.	Jean Beliveau, Mon.
Left Wing:	Bobby Hull, Chi.	Frank Mahovlich, Tor.
Right Wing:	Ken Wharram, Chi.	Gordie Howe, Det.

AWARDS

Hart Trophy — Jean Beliveau, Mon.
Lady Byng Trophy — Ken Wharram, Chi.
Norris Trophy — Pierre Pilote, Chi.
Calder Trophy — Jacques Laperriere, Mon.
Vezina Trophy — Charlie Hodge, Mon.

PLAYOFF RESULTS

Semi-Finals:	Toronto over Montreal,	4 games to 3
	Detroit over Chicago,	4 games to 3
Finals:	Toronto over Detroit,	4 games to 3

Stanley Cup Winning Goal: Andy Bathgate, Tor.

ALL-STAR TEAMS

	1st Team	2nd Team
Goal:	Roger Crozier, Det.	Charlie Hodge, Mon.
Defense:	Pierre Pilote, Chi.	Bill Gadsby, Det
Defense:	Jacques Laperriere, Mon.	Carl Brewer, Tor.
Center:	Norm Ullman, Det.	Stan Mikita, Chi.
Left Wing:	Bobby Hull, Chi.	Frank Mahovlich, Tor.
Right Wing:	Claude Provost, Mon.	Gordie Howe, Det.

AWARDS

Hart Trophy — Bobby Hull, Chi.
Lady Byng Trophy — Bobby Hull, Chi.
Norris Trophy — Pierre Pilote, Chi.
Calder Trophy — Roger Crozier, Det.
Vezina Trophy — Johnny Bower & Terry Sawchuk, Tor.
Conn Smythe Trophy — Jean Beliveau, Mon.

PLAYOFF RESULTS

Semi-Finals:	Chicago over Detroit,	4 games to 3
	Montreal over Toronto,	4 games to 2
Finals:	Montreal over Chicago,	4 games to 3

Stanley Cup Winning Goal: Jean Beliveau, Mon.

1965-66

FINAL STANDINGS

	W	L	T	PTS
Montreal	41	21	8	90
Chicago	37	25	8	82
Toronto	34	25	11	79
Detroit	31	27	12	74
Boston	21	43	6	48
New York	18	41	11	47

LEADING SCORERS

	G	A	PTS
Bobby Hull, Chi.	54	43	97 (Art Ross)
Stan Mikita, Chi.	30	48	78
Bobby Rousseau, Mon.	30	48	78
Jean Beliveau, Mon.	29	48	77
Gordie Howe, DeT	29	46	75

Most Penalty Minutes:	Reggie Fleming, Bos./N.Y. 166
Best Goals Against Avg:	Johnny Bower, Tor. 2.25
Most Shutouts:	Roger Crozier, Det. 7

ALL-STAR TEAMS

	1st Team	2nd Team
Goal:	Glenn Hall, Chi.	Gump Worsley, Mon.
Defense:	Jacques Laperriere, Mon.	Allan Stanley, Tor.
Defense:	Pierre Pilote, Chi.	Pat Stapleton, Chi.
Center:	Stan Mikita, Chi.	Jean Beliveau, Mon.
Left Wing:	Bobby Hull, Chi.	Frank Mahovlich, Tor.
Right Wing:	Gordie Howe, Det.	Bobby Rousseau, Mon.

1966-67

FINAL STANDINGS

	W	L	T	PTS
Chicago	41	17	12	94
Montreal	32	25	13	77
Toronto	32	27	11	75
New York	30	28	12	72
Detroit	27	39	4	58
Boston	17	43	10	44

LEADING SCORERS

	G	A	PTS
Stan Mikita, Chi.	35	62	97 (Art Ross)
Bobby Hull, Chi.	52	28	80
Norm Ullman, Det.	26	44	70
Ken Charram, Chi.	31	34	65
Gordie Howe, DeT	25	40	65

Most Penalty Minutes:	John Ferguson, Mon. 177
Best Goal Against Avg:	Denis DeJordy, Chi. 2.46
Most Shutouts:	Ed Giacomin, N.Y. 9

ALL-STAR TEAMS

	1st Team	2nd Team
Goal:	Ed Giacomin, N.Y.	Glenn Hall, Chi.
Defense:	Pierre Pilote, Chi.	Tim Horton, Tor.
Defense:	Harry Howell, N.Y.	Bobby Orr, Bos.
Center:	Stan Mikita, Chi.	Norm Ullman, Det.
Left Wing:	Bobby Hull, Chi.	Don Marshall, N.Y.
Right Wing:	Ken Wharram, Chi.	Gordie Howe, Det.

1965-66 Continued

AWARDS

Hart Trophy — Bobby Hull, Chi.
Lady Byng Trophy — Alex Delvecchio, Det.
Norris Trophy — Jacques Laperriere, Mon.
Calder Trophy — Brit Selby, Tor.
Vezina Trophy — Gump Worsley/Charlie Hodge, Mon.
Conn Smythe Trophy — Roger Crozier, Det.

PLAYOFF RESULTS

Semi-Finals:	Montreal over Toronto,	4 games to 0
	Detroit over Chicago,	4 games to 2
Finals:	Montreal over Detroit,	4 games to 2

Stanley Cup Winning Goal: Henri Richard, Mon.

1966-67 Continued

AWARDS

Hart Trophy — Stan Mikita, Chi.
Lady Byng Trophy — Stan Mikita, Chi.
Norris Trophy — Harry Howell, N.Y.
Calder Trophy — Bobby Orr, Bos.
Vezina Trophy — Glenn Hall/Denis DeJordy, Chi.
Conn Smythe Trophy — Dave Keon, Tor.

PLAYOFFS

Semi-Finals:	Toronto over Chicago,	4 games to 2
	Montreal over New York,	4 games to 0
Finals:	Toronto over Montreal,	4 games to 2

Stanley Cup Winning Goal: Jim Pappin, Tor.

HOCKEY HALL OF FAME MEMBERS PROFILED IN THIS BOOK:

Design and Production: Nick Pitt
Jacket Design: Dave Hader
Photographs: Harold Barkley
Photo Editor: Jacques Lumiere
Produced by: Shaftesbury Books/ Warwick Publishing, Toronto
Film and Separations: (CCGD) Creative Copy & Design, Toronto
Printing: Metropole Litho, Montreal

The Harold Barkley Archives
The collection of hockey photographs taken by Harold Barkley
spans the period from 1948 to 1972. It includes over 3000 large format
colour transparencies and 2000 black & white prints.
Inquiries to Warwick Publishing, Toronto